PERFORMING WAGNER

A Singer's Perspective
on the Major Tenor Roles

PERFORMING WAGNER

A Singer's Perspective
on the Major Tenor Roles

Stephen Gould
with **F. Peter Phillips**

With a Foreword by
Katharina Wagner

TOCCATA PRESS

First published in 2024 by Toccata Press
© 2024 by the estate of Stephen Gould and by F. Peter Phillips

All rights reserved. No part of this publication may be reproduced or transmitted in any form or by any means, electronic or mechanical, including but not limited to photocopy, recording, or any information storage or retrieval system without prior permission from the copyright holder or publisher.

British Library Cataloguing in Publication Data
A catalogue record for this book is available from the British Library.

ISBN 978-0-907689-41-6

Set in 11 on 12 point Minion Pro by Kerrypress Ltd
Printed and bound in Great Britain

Contents

Foreword	*Katharina Wagner*	7
Introduction	*F. Peter Phillips*	9
Acknowledgements		13
I Tannhäuser		15
II Tristan		33
III *The Ring of the Nibelung*		49
Loge		51
Siegmund		56
Siegfried in *Siegfried*		59
Siegfried in *Götterdämmerung*		68
IV Lohengrin and Erik		77
V Parsifal		87
VI Working with Conductors and Stage Directors		99
VII A Word on Technique		111
Epilogue: Colleagues remember Stephen Gould		127
Lise Davidsen		129
Markus Eiche		131
Catherine Foster		133
Ekaterina Gubanova		135
Tomasz Konieczny		136
Petra Lang		138
Tichina Vaughn		140
Michael Volle		141
Discography		143
Index of Operas and Roles		147
General Index		151

List of Illustrations

Stephen Gould in 2015	11
The historical Tannhäuser, as portrayed in the Codex Manesse	18
Joseph Tichatschek as Tannhäuser and Wilhelmine Schröder-Devrient as Venus in the premiere of *Tannhäuser* on 19 October 1845	20
Stephen Gould as Tannhäuser, Bayreuth Festival, 2022	22
Stephen Gould as Tannhäuser as clown, Bayreuth Festival, 2022	25
Tannhäuser, Act I, Semper Oper, Dresden, 2010: Stephen Gould and Tichina Vaughn	26
Tobias Kratzer's 2019 production of *Tannhäuser* at Bayreuth, 2022	29–30
Catherine Foster as Isolde and Stephen Gould as Tristan, Bayreuth Festival, 2022	41
Stephen Gould as Tristan, Bayreuth Festival, 2022	42
'Great Isoldes': Iréne Theorin, Evelyn Herlitzius and Petra Lang	47
Stephen Gould as Siegfried in *Götterdämmerung*, Bayreuth Festival, 2022	71
Götterdämmerung, Act III, Bayreuth Festival, 2022: Simone Schröder (Flosshilde), Stephen Gould (Siegfried), Lea-Ann Dunbar (Woglinde) and Stephanie Houtzeel (Wellgunde)	75
Stephen Gould as Lohengrin, Semper Oper, Dresden, 2006	85
Parsifal, Act III, Semper Oper, Dresden, 2005: Evelyn Herlitzius (Kundry), Stephen Gould (Parsifal) and Kurt Rydl (Amfortas)	96–97
Robert Carsen, Patrice Chéreau, Stefan Herheim and Tobias Kratzer	108
Franco Corelli and Magda Olivero	115
Wolfgang Windgassen and Jan Hendrick Rootering	119
Franz Grundheber	121
Franz Völker, Sándor Kónya, Peter Seiffert and Klaus Florian Vogt	122
Ludwig and Malwine Schnorr von Carolsfeld in the title roles of the original production of *Tristan und Isolde* in 1865	124

Foreword

Katharina Wagner

It is both a pleasure and an honour for me to contribute a foreword to this book by the singer Stephen Gould, who was also my close friend.

We knew each other for more than twenty years now, and worked together personally in my Bayreuth production of *Tristan und Isolde* – a wonderful experience. Stephen was one of the outstanding singing personalities of our time and was often – and rightly – called a 'long-distance runner'.

Who would ever have thought that the baritone and singer of musicals, with more than 3,000 performances of Andrew Lloyd Webber's *The Phantom of the Opera* to his credit, would become one of the most sought-after heroic tenors of our time?

In addition to the Wagner roles of Erik, Lohengrin, Parsifal, Siegfried, Siegmund, Tannhäuser and Tristan, Stephen also performed such extremely demanding roles as Florestan, Paul (*Die tote Stadt*), The Emperor (*Die Frau ohne Schatten*), Bacchus (*Ariadne auf Naxos*) and Otello. Always a positive person and a connoisseur, Stephen Gould possessed a remarkable vocal gift, irrepressible curiosity and the highest professionalism when dealing with his colleagues.

Stephen himself said that, for him, Wagner was not merely entertainment, but meditation – a mantra. At Bayreuth, Stephen Gould was one of the outstanding soloists from the 2006 season onwards, and he will forever remain part of our Festival family. He said Bayreuth was a place where he learned a lot and which was special to him. We in Bayreuth say the same about him.

In deep admiration.

Katharina Wagner
Director, Bayreuth Festival

Introduction
F. Peter Phillips

In 2006 I had the immense pleasure of attending the *Ring* cycle in Bayreuth that featured a young American singer in the role of Siegfried. I recognised his name – Stephen Gould – because I was serving on the Board of Directors of the Richard Wagner Society of New York and, several years before, the Society had given a (very modest) grant to Mr Gould to enable him to go to Europe for some auditions. And here he was on the Bayreuth stage!

I loved the performance. He was energetic and risk-taking. He was sensitive to the lyricism of the Forest Scene, blasting in the power of the Forging Scene, and sang farewell to Brünnhilde with a romance that few dying Siegfrieds can muster. He also was wearing one of the ugliest fat-suit costumes I had ever had the misfortune to witness on any stage, which endeared him to me all the more.

Two years later I was visiting Vienna for business and realised not only that the Staatsoper was offering *Siegfried*, but that the title role was being played by none other than Stephen Gould. This time I mustered my courage, left a note at the stage door purporting to represent the Wagner Society of New York and invited him to a post-performance dinner. And that was the start of our friendship. Since then, we had many a dinner in many a city as our travels periodically intersected, and we enjoyed each other's company very much.

During the 2020–21 Covid pandemic, I proposed to Stephen that we engage in a project to collect his thoughts on the experience of performing the nine major Wagner tenor roles: Erik in *Der fliegende Holländer*, Lohengrin, Parsifal, Tannhäuser, Tristan and four in *The Ring* (Loge, Siegfried in *Siegfried*, Siegfried in *Götterdämmerung* and Siegmund) – what they're like, and what he'd learned about how to do them well. My thinking was that many books have been written on the scores and the dramas, the theories and the interpretations of the roles and the works themselves; and many very entertaining memoirs and biographies have been written by actors, directors, conductors and others about their careers in Wagnerian production. But I had never encountered a systematic analysis of the performance challenges of these particular roles, written by someone who repeatedly performed them, for the purpose of sharing the experience of performance and the unique insights to be gained by putting the roles in your body and playing them out. I suggested that this kind of reportage would be of interest not only to younger tenors who are first trying on these roles, but also to the members of the audience like me, who have seen, been awed by, but never experienced what it is like to (for example) wrestle a bear, throttle a dwarf, forge a sword, kill a dragon, smash the spear shaft containing all the moral precepts of the universe, sever a warrior's armour, and sit back to consider how you are going to get through the next half-hour with a fresh-voiced Nina Stemme.

Stephen agreed, and this volume is the result of our labours. Stephen and I arranged conversations over the Zoom platform from Vienna, Bayreuth, Virginia, Munich and elsewhere, during which I would ask him about his performance experiences of one role at a time, and would record and transcribe his observations. We realised that a few topics came up from time to time that did not relate to a particular role, and so we prepared separate chapters on conductors, stage directors and the technique of singing this repertoire. But the heart of it was the preparation for, the experience of, and the reflections on performing these nine particular roles.

The voice of these chapters is Stephen's, and the content is (almost) entirely his.[1] When you read this book, you are hearing an internationally experienced performer speak about his encounters with these great characters before live audiences, collaborating with musical and theatrical colleagues of the highest calibre.

Over the course of any singing career, performing artists are drawn to reflect on the good fortune in learning from the great composers, conductors, designers, directors and colleagues with whom they've worked. Having the good fortune to build a sustained career has meant that they've had the opportunity to sing certain roles many times. And that has meant the unique gift of growing into them – discovering what's in the text and the score, why certain *fermate* or *rallentandi* are there, why certain words containing certain consonants are set to certain music at a certain tempo. And, of course, they've had the chance to share perceptions of stage action and musical content from the leading directors and conductors of their generation. As for what they learn from their peers – the stories in this volume shed moving insight into what happens when one sings with artists like Nina Stemme and Iréne Theorin.

---

[1] The footnotes are editorial, though note 6 on p. 28 is Stephen's, and is marked —SG for clarity.

Stephen Gould in 2015

Stephen emphasised that the observations in this book are his own. They are the uniquely subjective conclusions of a unique performer with uniquely subjective experiences. As with any great works of art, these roles can be played in many ways. Indeed, over a twenty-year career Stephen himself played them many ways, as he progressed in his own experience and insights. This is not the only way – or even the best way – to play these roles. It is just one performer's thoughts on how he learned to play them. Knowing Stephen as I came to know him, that sounds like a pretty good deal to me.

A few weeks after writing this Introduction, I received an e-mail from Stephen, who reported that, during the early days of rehearsal for the 2023 Bayreuth Festival, he was experiencing fatigue and some breathing issues. Over the next few days, he consulted doctors in Bayreuth and it became clear that he was subject to a serious health concern. His diagnostic procedures advanced, and he began to relinquish his roles in the Festival – first Tristan (to Clay Hilley), then Siegfried (to Andreas Schager) and finally Tannhäuser (to Klaus Florian Vogt). His medical issues became more pressing, and he returned to the United States in mid-July.

Stephen noted in his chapter on the role of Tannhäuser that he was the son of a preacher. He retained his religious convictions. His initial observation to me upon learning the seriousness of his medical condition was: 'What good is faith unless it is tested?'

In light of Stephen's death, on 19 September 2023, our book has become more timely, and even more meaningful. Very few performers have had the experiences that Stephen had, and none of them has had the occasion to share those experiences and to formulate, for the benefit of other artists and students of the art, the lessons learned. In this book an artist of stature has given insights into his art and, by extension, into the world of the singing actor. More to the point, he has provided an interpretive artist's insights into some of the great characters in Western dramatic literature.

I take considerable pride in having been part of a project that, owing entirely to Stephen Gould's generosity of spirit, will have lasting value.

Acknowledgements

The authors wish to acknowledge the support and assistance they received from Germán Bravo-Casas, Elaine Bromka, Hubertus Hermann, Roxanne Perryman, Julia Phillips, Stephen Wagley and Katharina Wagner.

The baritone Niall Hoskin – who has himself sung Wotan – read the text and caught a number of small errors, as did Barry Millington of the UK Wagner Society, and the index was compiled by Tom Corfield; my thanks to all three gentlemen.

For permission to use copyright photographs, I am grateful to the Bayreuth Festival for those on pp. 22, 25, 29, 30, 41, 42, 71 and 75, and to Matthias Creutzinger for those on pp. 26, 85, and 96–97. The portrait photographs introducing the tributes on pp. 129–41 were taken by James Hole (Lise Davidsen, p. 129), Uwe Arens (Catherine Foster, p. 133), Simon Pauly (Ekaterina Gubanova, p. 135), and Ann Weitz (Petra Lang, p. 138).

The chapter on the role of Tannhäuser appeared in the August 2021 issue of *Wagner News*, a publication of the UK Wagner Society.

It is a challenge to frame the thanks owed to Martin Anderson of Toccata Press. From the outset, he believed in us. His taste has been impeccable, his editing professional and his care has infused every page. Beyond that, however, he worked feverishly to get at least a proof of the book in Stephen's hands before his death; suggested the Epilogue section as an opportunity for Stephen's colleagues to express themselves; and provided personal as well as professional support to me throughout. I acknowledge his gifts and thank him for being a *mensch*.

F. Peter Phillips
Montclair, New Jersey
7 February 2024

I
Tannhäuser

Many people sense that *Tannhäuser* has 'too much God in it', that it has too much religious (especially Christian) implication to it. I don't think Wagner intended there to be religious implications, but in all his works he certainly intended spiritual exploration. And this is what we have here.

The role appealed to me the first time I heard it, because there does seem to be a lot of not only Christian but also Catholic reference. I grew up as a Nazarene minister's son, Wesleyan Methodist tradition. So I was prepared to attack this piece literally. And, if you take it literally, it's pretty carnal and pretty anti-Catholic. The structure of *Tannhäuser* is a mediaeval religious minnesinger[1] play. So it's helpful to start with just the bones.

In the very first scene, Tannhäuser says he wants his 'freedom'. But later he says he wants his 'salvation'. The interpreter of the role must focus on these ideas, and the spiritual journey that is implied by that change of ambition, to find the first key to performing it.

Tannhäuser has spent only sexual time with Venus – he has explored pure sensuality. Any minister's son knows that sometimes you push the envelope in the opposite direction. So Tannhäuser left his life of chivalry to enter a life of sensuality. Fine. But then why does Tannhäuser want to leave the Venusberg? When I first sang the role, I went along with the accepted story: that sex after a time gets boring and sensuality has its limits. I thought I understood both the spiritual side and the sensual side. But later, what was appealing to me was a different duality: this feeling of the outsider pitted against society. Tannhäuser, like Peter Grimes, is a great emotional role for me because they both had this setting of 'society oppressing the individual'.

We see Tannhäuser as somebody who is rejecting the (supposedly) chaste and ordered society and then going off to experience the sensual and chaotic. He discovers that neither chastity nor sensuality is the answer. Indeed, for him (in a presage of Tristan), it turns out that nothing is the answer.

In the mediaeval story we have in Tannhäuser a true minnesinger, whose job was to sing his own version of history. Some of them were able to challenge the court, like a court jester, without supposedly crossing the line. We get a glimpse of what Tannhäuser must have been like, before his visit to the Venusberg, when, at the end of Act I, the Landgrave cautions him

---

[1] A *Minnesänger* (minnesinger) was a poet/musician of the twelfth- to fourteenth-century Germany who wrote and performed on the topic of courtly love (*minne*). Minnesingers wrote and performed their own songs in open court, publicly embellishing and validating chivalric concepts of love.

The historical Tannhäuser (fl. 1245–65), as portrayed in the Codex Manesse (c. 1300–40), an anthology of the works of 135 minnesingers, each illustrated with a miniature 'portrait'

that, welcome as he is in the Wartburg, '*Zwietracht und Streit sei abgetan*'.[2] So clearly, Tannhäuser's behaviour as a courtier strained some people's expectations of propriety.

When we first encounter him, Tannhäuser is not rebelling against the strictures of the court. On the contrary, he wants to *leave* a world where everything is permitted, even if that means *returning to* a world where some things are simply not allowed. And it's a 'flee from' decision, not a 'go to' decision. When he leaves the Venusberg, Tannhäuser is clearly ambivalent as to whether the Wartburg is where he wants to be. He's just grateful that he's out of the black hole that was the Venusberg. He is certainly not trying to find the Virgin Mary, and he has not abandoned his earlier scepticism of the lords and ladies. What makes him stay in the Wartburg is Elisabeth.

It's a Christian concept that Tannhäuser has been redeemed through the sacrifice of Elisabeth. And I used to accept that construct when I first prepared to perform the character. But as I've continued to sing it, I'm coming to the conclusion that the question he is trying to answer is not whether Elisabeth can redeem him of his sin – indeed, I'm not sure that Tannhäuser even considers himself sinful, or in need of redemption. Rather, he is forced to confront the question whether redemption is even possible. (Wagner takes the question even further with *Tristan*, where the question is whether two people, irrespective of their moral condition, can ever truly come together in this life.)

For one thing, I don't think Elisabeth is accurately perceived as a chaste and pious wallflower. I think she's a real flesh-and-blood human being with whom Tannhäuser did have a relationship, perhaps a little more than the Landgrave would have thought. Early on, I realised there was quite a bit of past between the two of them. After '*Dich, teure Halle*,' when she sees him, she's embarrassed and says 'you can't see me here'. He asks why and realises that she already has responded to some of the things that he, at the time, had not yet discovered himself. Later on, she talks about how exciting it was. But it's more than just exciting. The music changes and she says: '*O helfet mir, dass ich das Rätsel meines Herzens löse!*'[3] And Tannhäuser, listening to this, becomes excited himself. Before he left the Wartburg, when he was

---

[2] 'Let strife and conflict be dismissed'. The mythical Venusberg had been a topos in German folk literature since the later Middle Ages and had become associated with the name of Tannhäuser – a genuine historical figure from the mid-thirteenth century – by the sixteenth century. The Wartburg, by contrast, is a real place – a mediaeval castle built on a cliff overlooking the town of Eisenach, in Thuringia, and now a tourist attraction. The name Elisabeth is also historically linked with the Wartburg: the princess Elisabeth of Hungary (1207–31) was sent there as a four-year-old child, to be betrothed to Ludwig IV, Margrave of Thuringia; the marriage took place when she was fourteen, but she was widowed six years later and died at the age of 24. She was canonised in 1235.

[3] 'Oh, help me solve the riddle of my heart!'

Joseph Tichatschek as Tannhäuser and Wilhelmine Schröder-Devrient as Venus in the premiere of Tannhäuser *on 19 October 1845 (engraving by Paul Tischbein)*

a court singer, Elizabeth didn't say: 'Oh you sing so pretty'. No, she was listening to Tannhäuser's words. She heard something that was sensual and exciting and that was causing her to become aroused. Now, upon meeting her anew, Tannhäuser thinks at that moment that she may be ready to go in this direction with him. And for the first time Tannhäuser realises this isn't just a child that he had been flirting with – and maybe went a little too far with. She's not this pure little wallflower. And considering where Tannhäuser himself has just come from, he is primed to perceive her erotic agency.

Later on, she starts talking about how she missed him, and she asks where Tannhäuser went. He can't say (or won't), but she already knew a little about where he was going. And now, he's been to the Venusberg – he's been as far as the human can go in terms of pure decadence, sexual energy, no taboos, no society, no limit. Moreover, learning this about Elisabeth, he now no longer cares whether he destroys this stilted and structured society, when given the opportunity to do so during the song contest. He now realises that Elisabeth – his intended audience – already understands at least a little of what he's about to say.

Similarly, in the recent Bayreuth production directed by Tobias Kratzer, the idea that Elisabeth causes her own death takes her out of the Catholic 'pure virgin' realm. This is what has confused people for so long, when they assume that the story of Tannhäuser is told in a Catholic religious context. It's not.

The Pope can't absolve Tannhäuser. If the Pope can't do that, then religion is inadequate to speak to Tannhäuser's condition. Wagner has very cleverly created this divergence between Venus and Elisabeth/Mary and the story is that the very structure that Wagner creates doesn't work; it's not the answer to the question that's posed. Either Elisabeth is a passive sacrificial lamb or Elisabeth is an active defender and participant. I suggest it's the latter. She joins Tannhäuser in his spiritual quest and in their shared fate.

We come now to the experience of performance. All this is interesting to discuss and muse upon, but it has practically no utility to the performer. Standing in the wings, the actor doesn't prepare in order to deal with backstories – he deals with what is at stake right now, the choices the character must make. And, right now, Tannhäuser needs to leave the Venusberg.

And we must think of the now, not of the later. You might allow yourself, while standing in the wings during the overture, to acknowledge that, in the course of the next four hours, your character will make a series of decisions that will result in his death. But this kind of thinking is not helpful to the performer – indeed, at best it makes you cerebral, and at worst paralyses

Stephen Gould as Tannhäuser, Bayreuth Festival, 2022

I: Tannhäuser

you and denies you the sudden, unplanned spontaneity that is an attribute of the character and, indeed, of the art of performance. And from that perspective, from the moment you step onstage at the start of the play, it is only this: 'I can't tolerate this anymore. I have to find a way to get out of this room. It is a living, eternal death'. That is the only way you can start.

The more I perform it, the more I realise that this mental and emotional state is the thread that runs through the experience of performing the entire role: needing to get out. Look at what he says and does: nowhere that Tannhäuser finds himself is satisfactory, or even tolerable, to him. Be it the Venusberg, the Wartburg, Rome or the open fields – he constantly needs to get out.

So in the first scene you say to yourself, what do I have to do to get this woman to let me go? Because you can't get out of there without her permission. And as you begin to deal with her, you realise that the only way to accomplish this is if she becomes so angry that she throws you out. So the objective of the first scene is to piss off Venus. And that's why each of the strophes builds. At first, 'I sing your praises my love, the love of my life, and so on. *Doch* [Yet].... I'm mortal, you're not, I have all these constraints, it's really getting old for me, I can't just have pleasure, I want to get back to where occasionally there is pain and remorse, and so on. So please won't you let me go?' And she responds, oh, what are you saying? And he gets more emphatic in the second strophe. He still starts off praising her, stroking her, but this time he's more direct: '*Göttin, lass' mich ziehn!*'[4] And she gets in a rage and they go back and forth with each other. Then finally, he gets explicit and insulting: 'Once I go, I will never come back to you. I would never come back to this'. And that's when she finally says '*Zieh hin*'. Go back to your terrible world. Go back to where they didn't accept you, where they had no sensuality whatsoever, where they ridiculed you and they controlled you and they had you under their thumb. Go back to the life you fled from in disgust. When he insists, she curses him: you will never find your goal, your salvation. That's why he shouts that he will find his salvation in Mary. And that's the one thing Venus can't stand, the Virgin Mary. And that's why he is thrown out. Mission accomplished.

Now, in truth, I strongly doubt that he really believes he will be redeemed from sin through the good offices of the Virgin Mary. His purpose, as you recall, is to get Venus angry, not to make religious professions. He's performative by nature, a *Minnesinger*. He uses words, music, action, to get a reaction out of people. And he succeeds, and wakes up outside of the Wartburg with a shepherd tooting a recorder. As we've discussed, he's not

---

[4] 'Goddess, let me go!'

comfortable there for a variety of reasons and is ambivalent about rejoining the court. The thing that changes his mind is Wolfram's naming Elisabeth. *That* is worth pursuing. So he stays.

He's open to the possibility that the Wartburg and Elisabeth might be a good place for him, but hardly enthusiastic. His first scene in Act II with Elisabeth is a wondrous discovery, as we've noted already, of Elizabeth's perceived openness to sensuality and passion. But then comes the song contest.

Any time one experiences what one thinks is a higher level of knowledge or wisdom or perception, it's difficult to go back and listen to people talk about something that they don't know anything about. In the song contest, when the theme is announced, we have the *Minnesinger* coming out in all of them. The trouble is, the rest of the men think of courtly love and Tannhäuser just plain doesn't.

Yes, agrees the court, we're all going to sing – because singing is a higher form than just speaking the words themselves and it is a supposedly higher form of communication. So, as a singer, each of them is used to getting up and expounding on it, to see which of them, through song, can evoke the greater wisdom to the subject. That's the point of the competition. But Tannhäuser, in a certain sense, has been trapped by his own hubris. He figures, 'the nature of love? You have to be joking'. On that topic he's a professional among amateurs, isn't he? He's already experienced every degradation, every limit to what he would call love – sensual, spiritual, whatever. So when he starts this competition, it's almost impossible for him to listen to lesser beings (in his mind) expound upon something they don't know anything about.

Tannhäuser is a recently returned visitor to courtly manners and, inured as he is to a lifestyle of sexual libertinism, he doesn't consider there is a cost to saying aloud truths that others only whisper. If one were analysing the character, one might sit back and think, hmmm, I don't think this is going to go well. But not as a performer. A performer doesn't analyse; he just does. And Tannhäuser is a performer.

Tannhäuser-the-performer is in the emotion of the moment so much, so deeply, so exclusively, that Tannhäuser-the-courtier doesn't realise the effect of what he's going to say. As we know, it doesn't go well at all, does it? But does Tannhäuser-the-divided-*persona* even realise what he's done?

Initially when I was performing the role, I would immediately regret the impulsive, public confession of living with Venus, and act accordingly. But later this changed.

Interestingly, once living with Venus is invoked, Wagner has all the women of the chorus immediately run out. The men stay, and they don't

Stephen Gould as Tannhäuser, Bayreuth Festival, 2022, portrayed as a clown in Tobias Krazter's production, premiered in 2019. The slogan – 'Free in your desire, free in your action, free in your enjoyment' – was a statement made by Wagner in 1849, during his period as a revolutionary.

Tannhäuser, *Act I, Semper Oper, Dresden, 2010:*
Stephen Gould as Tannhäuser and Tichina Vaughn as Venus

stay in order to lecture Tannhäuser or to learn cool stories of life with Venus; they draw their swords. They stay to kill him. It never occurred to me until much later that that's the reason Elisabeth cries out in protection – that she's the only woman left onstage, and it is left to her, alone, to intervene.

So as my experience in the role grew deeper, and my willingness to explore this frightening moment became perhaps a bit more enabled, I experimented by continuing this arrogance in the face of the death that I thought was coming to me from the men, until Elisabeth screamed 'Stay your hands'. And it was only at that moment I begin to understand. It's shocking to Tannhäuser to find that not all the women left – that Elisabeth stayed. She is still there. And she says, I'm the one that has been offended here, not all of you in this room. That's the great moment of realisation. That's when Tannhäuser realises: what have I done? Hurt the only person in my life who matters? This is not what I wanted to happen. He wishes then, for the first time, that he had never come back.

We should be clear about this. We are not talking regret for what he said or did. We're talking regret for what is happening *to him*, and especially *to her*. I don't think you can be remorseful for living on a higher plane of awareness. You can regret that you went too far, and certainly you can regret hurting someone who merits protection rather than harm. And that's what happens at this moment, for the first time, falling on his moral sensibility

I: Tannhäuser

like a ton of bricks. Tannhäuser doesn't regret the words; he regrets the harm to Elisabeth. Society doesn't matter to him; he is and always was an anarchist. It's what he's done to her.

Remember that Tannhäuser didn't want to *go to* the Wartburg; what he wanted to do was to *leave* the Venusberg. And similarly now, he doesn't want to *go to* Rome; he needs to *leave* the Wartburg. Where to? With Rome, there is at least a possibility that he could recover Elisabeth. In any event, without Rome, there is no chance at all. So, '*Nach Rom*' ('To Rome').

That reason, that motivation if you will, is one that I have always found by far the most supportive to choose to play. When I hear the Landgrave say there are pilgrims, you should travel to Rome, I've always played that as, What good can that possibly do? It's a reaction: OK, I'm going to go and perhaps, if I show enough remorse I can be redeemed. But Tannhäuser is not suddenly pious. He is not actually enthusiastic about that. I don't think he's seeking religious or even moral salvation; he's seeking Elisabeth.

There's then this long choral finale, and look at Tannhäuser's lines: How am I supposed to find it? Do I fall in the dust? Do I beat my breast? Throw ashes on my face? Repentance doesn't come easy for this man. I want repentance, perhaps, but what the pilgrims offer me is ritual, it's dogma. You don't repent because the prayer book says so. But how does Tannhäuser manage that? All of Tannhäuser's lines are 'If only I…', 'If…'. Does Tannhäuser really think that he should say ten Hail Mary's and Elisabeth will return? He's a confused guy but he's not that delusional.

Now we come to Act III – the real despair. Tannhäuser's done everything. He's marched to Rome without shoes on, filthy clothes, crawling. While others were giving prayers, he said that he was unworthy. The sun bore down on him. He's in a terrible state in terms of doing all these penitential things. And then when he gets there…

As I say, I've always played the end of Act II onstage assuming that it's not going to work. The music in the Paris version[5] is very, very chromatic and it's very long. It's almost Schoenberg. And I like that music because, in my head, I know: This is not going to work, but for Elisabeth… *Nach Rom!*

And now the Pope says, I'll forgive everybody in this room, but not you. Remember where we started? That some people find *Tannhäuser* too religious? *The Pope withholds forgiveness?!* Can you imagine anything more extraordinarily anti-religious? And I think Wagner did it on purpose. Considering his state of mind at the end of Act II, I don't think Tannhäuser

---

[5] *Tannhäuser* was premiered in Dresden in 1845, and in 1861, with the promise of a performance at the Opéra de Paris that Wagner thought would bring him much-needed attention, he prepared a revised version of the score, making a large number of changes, chief of which was the insertion of a ballet (required by French operatic tradition) into Act I – the Venusberg Bacchanale.

is in the least surprised that the Pope rejects him and throws him back into the world without the possibility of redemption. The Pope is saying that Tannhäuser has no hope, either in the Venusberg or in the world. And to that conclusion, I believe both Tannhäuser and the Pope can agree.

Think about it: if the Pope had demanded of Tannhäuser, what is the sin you want to be forgiven, what would Tannhäuser have said? I think he would have no answer. I don't think Tannhäuser thinks he has sinned, at least not against the Pope or God. So his bitterness when he enters the stage in Act III is not that he has been rejected by the Pope. That's not news. It is that he remains guilty of harming Elisabeth and now he has no place left to go, anywhere, to atone.

When we see him enter in Act III, Tannhäuser is a broken man. Once again, he doesn't expect to return to the Wartburg; he just couldn't stand to be in Rome anymore. He's in a cycle of hell; the only outcome he can articulate is annihilation through Venus. And what stops him? The word 'Elisabeth' again. And again, it's Wolfram who says it. If it's true that Tannhäuser was not affirmatively seeking to return to his former society, then it's purely by accident that the returning Tannhäuser stumbles upon Wolfram.

Some people say that a dramatic character can be encapsulated by a single gesture. If that's so, then Tannhäuser's gesture is rejection and flight. Every time Tannhäuser is challenged, he runs away. He's trying to run away from the Venusberg; he's trying to run away from his old society but is pulled back by Elisabeth; he doesn't want to go to Rome and then when he doesn't receive absolution he runs away and stumbles across Wolfram. And now here he is. His state is as follows: I can't be absolved, I'll never be absolved, there is no place in society for me, there's no human love in my life nor will there ever be. There is only one conclusion: I'm going back to Venus. And then Tannhäuser either sees or hears what Elisabeth has done and realises that Venus is not an option either. In response, he dies.

That's the moment of alternative annihilation, where there really is no place left to go – not even to Venus. I find it interesting that the Pope says you'll never be absolved, and at the end of the first scene of Act I Venus says you'll never be able to come back. And yet here she is, at the end of the play, answering his call.[6] Yet rather than that end, he accepts the ultimate end – death.

This business of salvation coming through a woman is a little abrasive, perhaps, to contemporary sensibilities. I see what happens to Tannhäuser,

---

[6] The first time I did Tannhäuser, in Linz, the director wanted to do the very first version, where Venus never came back – Tannhäuser imagined it. She never came back to sing. So I learned the ending differently from what we now know. Tannhäuser is hearing her but she's not there. If that's the original content, I like to think I've kept that in my own interpretation – that it's all in my mind. This clears things up a little bit. —SG

Three outsiders in Tobias Kratzer's 2019 production of Tannhäuser at Bayreuth, 2022, Act II: the drag queen 'Le Gateau Chocolat', Stephen Gould as Tannhäuser and Manni Laudenbach as a silent character, Oskar

Tobias Kratzer's 2019 production of Tannhäuser, *Bayreuth, 2022: Manni Laudenbach as Oskar (silent role), Ekaterina Gubanova as Venus and Stephen Gould as Tannhäuser*

I: Tannhäuser

however, not as sacrificial salvation but as ultimate self-realisation; as Tannhäuser's finally being given to understand that, for him, there is only Elisabeth. And if she has 'saved' him, she has done so by modelling self-annihilation. She has concluded that she can't live. He now realises that too. It is only through death that Tannhäuser's soul and his circumstance will finally meet. She could not live in a world without Tannhäuser, and she models the strength to die. She shows him the way.

Wagner closes by giving us a beautiful (and theatrical) metaphor: the reason the leaves grow on the Pope's staff, and on the walking sticks of all of the Pilgrims, is not because of the Pope; it's because of Elisabeth. The Pope, in his dogmatic blindness, said it will never happen, and here – through the intercession of loving self-annihilation – we're seeing it happen before our very eyes.

The performance has ended. We're now in the dressing room, pooped. Let's look back on what we've done by performing *Tannhäuser*. At the beginning of the opera, we started by needing to get out of the room. We entered the great room of the court, and within minutes we needed to get out of that room. After painful and searching wandering, we discovered that we needed to get out of Rome, and eventually out of 'The Room' writ large, once and for all. We came to the conclusion that there is no there, there. And Elisabeth showed us the way. And we followed her.

I think Wagner writing this character is a gesture of self-therapy. Writing this work at the age of 32, Wagner poses to himself, through *Tannhäuser*, the urgent questions of the young creative artist. What is art and what is not? What are the boundaries of the artistic gesture?

What constraints does society impose on the artist, and which of these should be accepted, which overthrown? The performer approaching Tannhäuser this way opens limitless interpretive possibilities. Is he going to be a painter? A singer? Is he going to die at the end or not? Is Elisabeth a hybrid of Venus, a repentant Magdalen?

In the end, the whole point of *Tannhäuser*, for those brave enough to confront it, is that at the end of the rainbow there is nothing – that it is only through death that the ultimate resolution of these essential questions is found. Or perhaps we should talk not of death but of transformation of the human soul – the human essence – to a new form.

Sounds a little like *Tristan*…. Or perhaps an epic narrative with a repeating cycle…

II
Tristan

To many non-singers – and indeed to many performers – *Tristan und Isolde* occupies a place of awe. So great is its musical achievement that it has attained a kind of mystery status in performance. People cannot seem to hold it in their imaginations as a real thing – in particular, that the role of Tristan is something that one learns and performs as one does other roles. They don't see how it is possible that the score could have been written, or that the role could be sung.

The musical intervals between the notes of the vocal score frequently can't be heard clearly, so unfamiliar are they presented, so dense is the scoring and orchestration, and so powerful are the feelings that the music evokes. And the story of its aborted first rehearsals in Vienna, and the triumph and subsequent death of the first Tristan, Ludwig Schnorr von Carolsfeld,[1] feeds into this legend. It all combines to provoke a general sense of 'more than'. The work, the role, the event, all exist in myth, even though the work itself is right there in front of us, each time we open the score or attend a performance.

I don't disagree, frankly. Indeed, I think that's as it should be. The mythology of *Tristan* is an important key to performing the role. I don't think you should try to de-mystify the work.

People try to make sense of *Tristan* because the temptation for the 'serious' artist is to start from the practical side – both when you're performing it and when you're closely listening to it. We think that *Tristan und Isolde* is a story, that it has a plot, because it is an opera and operas tell stories. We latch on to the fact that it came out of historical sources that were ancient story fragments. We seek to go behind the legend.

But why would one seek to de-mystify *Tristan*? How does making it understandable take us to a better place? Isn't the mystical, mythical experience of watching *Tristan* the very thing that the work was intended to achieve – the very reason we return to it as audiences? Is not the content of the piece also the consequence of the piece – loss of narrative, loss of constraints, of reality, of quotidian concern? Submerging into a world that

---

[1] The premiere, planned for the Vienna Court Opera, was aborted after 70 rehearsals because the tenor, Alois Ander (1821–64), was unable to learn the role and the orchestra found the score too demanding. Attempts to mount productions in Dresden, Weimar and Prague also failed. The opera was finally premiered in Munich on 10 June 1865, but the Tristan, Ludwig Schnorr von Carolsfeld (1836–65), died on 21 July, only seven weeks after the premiere (and nineteen days after his 29th birthday), having sung only four public performances. Rumours blamed his death on the demands of the role; it was more probably caused by a chill caught on stage, perhaps exacerbated by Schnorr von Carolsfeld's weight.

is deeply felt but not in any cognitive sense understood? Why is it a bad thing that, at core, we can't understand *Tristan*? Not understanding it is, perhaps, the very place we need to be in order to hear it, and to perform it, at its fullest.

When I learned the role, I had a great advantage. I knew that performing Tristan would have to be timed towards the end of my career, but at the same time I wanted to learn it early enough that I still had the strength. My first Siegfried had been at Bayreuth, the centre of the Wagner world, and that perhaps had been a misjudgement. It exposed me to pressure and critical assessment too early in my understanding of this great, great role. Perhaps I should have done Siegfried first in a small theatre somewhere, to give me a chance to feel my way into it. So, when it came time to learn how to perform Tristan, I wanted to do it in a place where I could learn how to do it, how to become accustomed to the peculiar demands of the role, without these first efforts being internationally assessed.

To learn it, I worked over a period of maybe two-and-a-half years. And I want to emphasise that I was *working* on it during that extended period of time. It wasn't like once a week for a half hour; I was doing two- or three-hour sessions a day, especially in the final year. And to try it on, I found New National Theatre Tokyo – a good place with an excellent orchestra and an excellent conductor but quite a far distance from the European critics.

The role is, in fact, quite challenging to hear – to put in your ear – as you learn it. This is because the tonalities and the harmonies change so quickly. The intervals are often not diatonic, and the harmonic and metrical changes can be very abrupt. Several different tonalities come on top of each other, and you never know, as you try to learn the arc of a particular phrase, where it will settle. Musically it's brilliant, but if you're trying to memorise it, it can be fiendishly demanding.

So I found that it's the poetry that one needs to attend to carefully. The poetry tells you that it's not so much a story-opera as it is a symphony for voice. Understanding that distinction, and attending to the words carefully, helped me to absorb the role rather than simply 'learn' it. Once I learned to sing it, and took the next step of experiencing it in performance, I realised that I wasn't performing it for others – I was, in some strange way, merely *there* when it happened around me. I was experiencing it in much the same way the audience was, and I had the best seat in the house. I'm not so much singing this role as I am experiencing this myth. It was, and remains, an entirely unique experience.

As a listener, the same thing may happen to you. Yet many people approach the score with an intention of analysing it and thinking about it, almost creating a theology around it. For me it's gone well past where

II: Tristan

you study the motifs and you study the structure and you examine the metre and you study the harmonies and how much Schopenhauer is in this, and the critical analysis, and Wesendonck, and so on.[2] That part of my preparation didn't feed me. Indeed, in the end, now that I know the role, I realise that that's not the point. The point of it is to jump in, fully and almost without looking, and experience it on a visceral level. That's what I think Wagner meant when he said that if anyone truly heard the piece, they would go mad. What *Tristan* does is to invite you to let go of the world you are familiar with, and to cease to care whether you return to it.

For Schopenhauer, existence itself is the original sin. I'm not sure Wagner went quite so far, but he was trying to recognise that, as Buddhism taught him, there are compelling religious emotions that exist independent of theology. Roger Scruton wrote convincingly about this concept.[3] The core proposition that you have to accept, if you are going to perform it – if you are going to personify Tristan himself – is that *Tristan und Isolde* is not telling us a story; it is portraying, and inviting us to experience, a sequence of profound human emotions centred on the frustration of being alive and alone, and the attraction of death as a way to satisfy our need for connection with another human being. *Tristan* invites us to entertain the proposition that the true coming-together of two individual souls is the goal of life, but (paradoxically) cannot occur except in death, and that death is therefore not a termination of one's life into oblivion, but rather a release of one's soul into an eternal ocean of the sacred.

Wagner was at heart a storyteller, and this type of theatre was a departure for him. He engages in this non-narrative exercise only once more, in *Parsifal*. I hope you can intuit my meaning when I report that, during performance, I am the ultimate recipient, rather than the donor. I've gotten to the point that I don't consider myself a singer of Tristan. I'm not performing it; I am literally experiencing it myself. I have no responsibility to narrate the plot; I'm discovering the condition of yearning for connection through oblivion and release, myself.

---

[2] Wagner encountered Schopenhauer's philosophy in 1854 and it – especially *The World as Will and Representation* (1818) – was an important influence on the composition of *Tristan und Isolde*, which was triggered, in 1854, by Wagner's infatuation, and perhaps affair, with Mathilde Wesendonck (1828–1902).

[3] In Roger Scruton, *Death-devoted Heart: Sex and the Sacred in Wagner's 'Tristan und Isolde'* (Oxford University Press, Oxford, 2003), the author explains, for example, 'In desire we encounter sanctity, desecration, consecration and atonement; and by exalting desire into love we seek redemption. These religious ideas indicate no particular faith; they are retrieved *from the human experience itself*, by a drama that has the truth of our condition as its foremost controlling aim' (p. 54); and, 'Wagner is presenting in dramatic outline the image of man as his own redeemer. He is suggesting that we can achieve the transfiguration for which it is in our nature to yearn with no help from God' (p. 185).

A lot of singers are wrapped up in the voice. Understandable – they're singers, after all. But it's important for me to acknowledge that, to some, mine may not be the most beautiful voice. I may not display the most riveting masculine beauty for the stage. But the reason why I'm still here, being invited to sing Tristan in theatres around the world, is that I have learned with certain pieces (not all) to throw myself into it for my own discovery, my own voyage into myth, and the truths that come with myth.

It's there, by the way; I'm not making this up. One can sense a pervasive lack of control, a measure of impetuosity, throughout the score. It's as if Wagner himself didn't intend it, that he wanted to write something simple and easy to mount, and then it just got massively out of hand. The music seems almost unplanned, that it's pouring out by virtue of its own force. Wagner wrote experience rather than music, and he expected people to enter into the emotion rather than listen to the performance. The play opens with massive rage of Isolde, based on a motif that screams up and down in a jagged progress that is itself mad. It doesn't just depict fury; the music *is* fury.

Nor is this attribute limited to the music. As I say, learning the words was at least as exciting and revealing as learning the notes. I initially found the words in the early dialogue in Act II frankly incoherent. They seemed excessive, incomprehensible – an awkward confession to make if you are supposed to be performing them. And then over a period of time I let go, and just let myself enter into it. These lines are questions, yet are all really expressions of emotion, not someone seeking coherent answers. I discovered that Tristan frequently articulated statements that seemed practically nonsensical, but then three lines later Isolde would ask a question to which Tristan's previous statement would have been the answer. This is the conflation of space/time to which the Buddhist aesthetic gives license.

Then there is the additional challenge of accepting, and living in, Tristan's profound melancholy – an essential attribute of the character, almost to the level of a disorder. This comes from some of the mediaeval stories as well. Tristram, as a warrior in the Arthurian legend, was second in fierceness only to Lancelot. But Lancelot's bravery – of an almost indestructible nature – was due to his superior competence on the battlefield. Tristram's deadliness derived from the fact that he did not care whether he was killed. It didn't matter to him whether he died or not. He was almost looking for a way to die. It must have been a frightening thing to confront on the battlefield.

It's also revealing to note the number of times Tristan attempts – if not actively, at least passively – to invite death as affirmation. In the course of the play itself he does it several times: in the First Act he gives his sword to Isolde and invites her to kill him, and subsequently drinks what he

II: Tristan

understands to be poison; in the Second Act he successfully taunts Melot to stab him, suffering a mortal wound; and in the Third Act he rips off his own bandages, re-opens his wounds and prompts his own death. And before the play begins, we learn, as Tantris he had shared this very experience with her: that she recognised him, and knew him as the man who had killed her betrothed; that she was ready to kill him; and that he was ready to die.

With these predispositions – emotional rather than analytical, abandoning the expectation of sequential narrative in the lines you're given to sing, embracing myth and legend, experiential and death-affirming – let's now see what happens when you perform the role.

We first see Tristan staring out into the ocean, so detached that he is startled when he is approached by Kurwenal. Why is he doing this? The sea is so rich, isn't it? Other composers and painters and writers have used it because the sea is always the seat of deep and unattainable emotion. The sea also attracts the wanderer that Tristan is – the searcher, the one always seeking the furtive nature of being, and the nature of death. (As the piece progresses, Isolde comes to the same insight. I've always thought that the love of Tristan and Isolde is, at least in part, because they are the same souls on the same journey; it's just that, when the curtain rises, he is further along than she is in the voyage towards release.)

So there he is, staring at the sea. The only love he ever experienced in his life is down in the hold of the ship and he refuses even to look at her. They are an hour offshore, an hour before he is to deliver her to a loveless political marriage with aged King Marke, and he is giving navigational directions to the crew. But remember – this work is not always about love itself; it's about the journey through love towards death. Tristan already understands that in this life, in this plane of existence, there can be no love. It is only on the other plane, in the state of death, that lives truly come together. So when Kurwenal announces Brangäne, and Brangäne announces that Isolde commands Tristan's presence, he doesn't really respond. Tristan has resolved himself that Isolde does not understand, so he is willing to let matters run their course. He is trying to distance himself, if you will, from this absurd situation. He is also frankly frightened to approach Isolde directly, because he himself doesn't want to acknowledge the love between them. If he were to confront her, they both might become weak. So he refuses to come near her. I have played it this way – I send Kurwenal to brush them off, but when I hear what he says, I am embarrassed. Kurwenal is rude and insults the Irish princess. So Tristan is, in a sense, compelled to speak to her directly.

When Tristan walks through the door he is (of course) hoping that Isolde will not in any way show the love that he feels. You can be bitter towards someone and still show them that there is a deep connection. He offers her, again, the chance to kill him if he has so deeply offended her honour as she says he has. But does he really offer her his life? Earlier, when he was wounded as Tantris, she could have easily dispatched Tristan with few consequences. Now, if she were to kill him, Marke may have something to say about it. So is this an invitation to kill him or is it something else, some definitive gesture inviting them both to admit that the game is played out? (By the way, I think some people forget that part of the story: she is still the princess, and not fulfilling her duty to Marke will result in war and strife for her people. Rant as she may, she has played all her cards, and so has he.)

So much attention is given to the love potion. Does the potion make them come together? To me, the most exciting interpretive choice is to deny any agency whatsoever to the potion. In Katharina Wagner's production in Bayreuth in 2018, we dropped the potion on the floor and dealt with each other directly. Adopting this interpretation forces the two characters at that moment to acknowledge to each other, and no longer to deny, the naked truth of their condition. If they actually drink it, it still works fine – he wants to die and now at this last moment he is free to let her know what he feels. Having decided to end their lives, they take that moment to express the truth between them. But pouring it on the floor, instead of drinking it, is an even stronger statement: we are going to consummate this because we both see now that we are indelibly spiritually connected. We don't need the potion, and we will no longer deny the passion.

It must be admitted that Wagner himself is not completely clear about the dramatic import of the potion – neither here nor with the other magic potion, in *Götterdämmerung*. The potion that Siegfried drinks is, shall we say, selective; it may have caused him to forget Brünnhilde, but it did not make him into the deceptive human being he became in other respects. The point of the potion in *Tristan* is not the drinking of it – it is to precipitate the great moment of their mutual decision to succumb to love.

Another important point: they are more than carnally united. They are not going to have sex and produce children. Instead, they are going to create a single sacred unit. Admittedly, the music from that point to the end of the act is pounding, hasty, breathless. But that is the consequence of submission to spiritual ecstasy. In describing my joy in performing it, the potion plays a marginal role. Tristan ecstatically longs for release from the hell of existence. He knows that only in death will he experience connection, and if (as they think) they have swallowed a death potion, then they are going to die in passion. And again, if you stage it so to as to abjure the potion, the gesture is all the more startling: We are *not* going to die, *and* we nevertheless embrace and acknowledge our passionate spiritual connection.

II: Tristan 41

Catherine Foster as Isolde and Stephen Gould as Tristan, Bayreuth Festival, 2022

At the very end of the First Act, they have let themselves go to full experience. They don't know what will happen now. Then at the start of Act II you have the broad themes established, and as a performer you simply jump in. The emotion, the experience of this music, is new each time – as it should be if you really experience it.

By the time we get to Act II, there is no frenzied potion-induced energy to distract us. Yes, Tristan is rushing and, yes, the music is pounding. But he is rushing to the light. When she puts out the light, Tristan calls for it. That section is one of my least favourite moments in the entire piece, technically. (You go up to a high A on an *ee* vowel – not something to be sought after.) But I'm not sure it's meant to be beautiful – ecstasy is to be experienced, not described or illustrated. When the characters talk in mystical language in Act II, it's like the ocean we were talking about. I think of Tristan and Isolde in Act II as what happens to somebody when they get caught in a riptide. If you swim against that tide you will tire, you will drown, and you will die. What do you do in a riptide? You swim sideways and wait for help to come to you. You survive. You experience what it's like to be out there. And, of course, you hope that a shark doesn't kill you in the meantime.

Stephen Gould as Tristan, Bayreuth Festival, 2022

The first part of the duet is hasty, inquiring, challenging, exciting. They take up where they left off. And they start a circuitous layering on top of each other. It's almost like they are in parallel universes, signalling to each other. The dialogue is all temporally disjointed: He answers, and then a few lines later she asks the question. They are in different metres. Her tone is more accusing, his is more ecstatic. Then they slowly come together, '*O, nun waren wir Nachtgeweihte!*'[4] Then they come down to this sense of darkness, death, the 'real' world. Death is the transition to the real world for Tristan. They slowly come together, the ecstasy has gone down, and suddenly there is the undercurrent of the night. This is the calm, at '*O sink' hernieder, Nacht der Liebe*'[5]. Let's sink down into death, sink down into love, 'real' love. And there is a placidity, a unity of souls. And musically it comes together. Two people coming into one. But they are still not in 'harmony' in a diatonic sense. This is an emotional, not a physical, ecstasy. And once they finally have it together, he sings '*So stürben wir um ungetrennt…*'[6] And this is when she gets it. Then when it builds for the last time, '*Höchste Liebeslust*'[7] (the tenor, thank God, is not expected to sing the high C), they actually are on

---

[4] 'Oh, now we were dedicated to night!'

[5] 'Sink down, night of love'.

[6] 'O might we then die together'. The verb in that phrase has been the subject of textual debate, some commentators arguing for 'starben', a straight past indicative ('Thus we died'), suggesting that Tristan thinks that it has already happened; 'stürben', the subjunctive, makes death an end to be desired.

[7] 'Highest bliss of love'.

II: Tristan

the same note. They have come together, but not in the same octave. And that's when Melot rushes in with Marke.

There follows the most wonderful scene. To me, Tristan's confronting Marke should not be played with too much embarrassment or shame. Quite the contrary. I remember seeing the original Konwitschny[8] production in Munich with Waltraud Meier[9] and Siegfried Jerusalem,[10] and Kurt Moll[11] as Marke, and I loved what Meier did. They're confronted by Marke, why did you do this, how could you betray one who loved you. And Isolde has a look of ecstasy on her face. I loved that because then it makes so much sense when Tristan says to Marke, 'O König, das kann ich dir nicht sagen'.[12] (Notice by the way that Tristan says 'dir'. Strangely intimate, almost presumptuous, to refer to the king as 'dir'. Yet he says it because he is speaking the truth. Tristan is no longer in Marke's world of hierarchy and deference.)

Let's consider that wonderful, supremely expressive, moment. Is Tristan saying 'I don't know the answer to your question?' No. He is saying: 'What is happening can't be described using words. The thing you are asking us to tell you is something we ourselves can't comprehend. It is beyond articulation – indeed, it is beyond contemplation. It is only to be experienced'. And this is the moment that Tristan and Isolde are each at their best, because they both realise that this is the end. You can't go any further – not because they have been discovered, but because they have gone to the end of experience. This is why Tristan drops his sword and allows himself to be run through by Melot.

Notice that he addresses the rest of his explanation, not to Marke by way of response, but to Isolde by way of invitation. He says to her – not him – that he is going to the land of darkness where the sun doesn't shine – where he came from – a land of pre-birth. Will she follow him? Then his thoughts are broken (the music is so gorgeous there) and she responds yes, and the music has them kiss. This is their Liebestod, their finest and final hour together.

Then Melot is used as an agent of murder. Tristan purposely provokes Melot. (This is the only interpretation I can come up with or feel comfortable

---

[8] Peter Konwitschny (b. 1945) is the son of the conductor Franz Konwitschny; he produced *Tristan und Isolde* in Munich in 1998.

[9] German soprano and mezzo-soprano (b. 1956), particularly esteemed for her portrayal of Kundry, not least in the 1990s at Bayreuth, where she also sang Sieglinde in *Die Walküre* in 2000.

[10] Siegfried Jerusalem (b. 1940) began his musical career as a bassoonist but began his operatic career singing Lohengrin in 1976, first appeared at Bayreuth in 1977 and has since sung the major Wagner tenor roles around the world. He last sang at Bayreuth in 1999 as Tristan and now concentrates on the Lieder repertoire. He is also a master singer of Nuremberg in the strictest sense, in that he teaches at the College of Music there.

[11] German bass (1938–2017).

[12] 'Oh king, I cannot tell you that'.

with because, on the merits as a fighter, Tristan would be clearly the victor against Melot or for that matter anyone). Even Melot himself is shocked by it. Tristan intends to die then and there, and expects that Isolde will do the same. Neither happens, of course.

We learn everything we need to know about Isolde in Act I, but we learn everything we need to know about Tristan in Act III. Kareol is his place of birth. Tristan was always an outsider to Cornwall, a vassal pledged to Marke, not a member of the court. In the Bayreuth production in 2018, I adopted the idea that Act III takes place at the very brink of death – during, say, the last four minutes, as the brain is biologically dying. I'm on the ground in exactly the same manner as if I had been stabbed, but rather than seeing Melot and Marke I see my home, with my attendants around me. All the different episodes in the Act are Tristan's dying thoughts, his life projected before him, in the last moments of the death throe. It is his life described through his narrative of recollection when he is really, for all practical purposes, already dead.

The long monologue is divided into three separate narratives. I learned them that way, which was helpful because of necessity I needed to learn not only the music but the vocal pacing as well. It starts as Kurwenal tries to pull Tristan back into the life Tristan had been in. Tristan is reluctant to return, describing it as a lonely land. The second narrative describes the world of reality as a terrifying land, and the final narrative describes the hopelessness of all of it, until he learns that Isolde is coming. Tristan responds in delirious joy, not in hope that Isolde brings a cure; he just wants her to come so she will be with him, and so that they can both descend together into the next, true, land, as they had hoped to do at the end of Act II.

In my experience, the structure of these three narratives is critical to understanding the role – and also to being able to sing the Act, as a technical matter. They are different aspects of the same thing, and their interplay creates a conflict so fundamental that it can be resolved only in oblivion, in death. In the Munich Konwitschny production, Isolde actually goes and crosses the Veil of Maya, and there is Tristan ready to greet her. However you stage it, at the final B major chord, they have become one, just as they had foreseen.

Through all of the suffering Tristan experienced in his life, he was unable to find *transcendence* in death (as opposed to mere oblivion or extinction) until he was able to find love, spiritual union with another person. And in the passage at the end of the third section of the narrative we find the only lyrical solo passage in the role. He accepts an almost childlike understanding of what serenity is, and then associates it with Isolde:

sie führt mir letzte Labung zu.

II: Tristan

Ach, Isolde! Isolde! Wie schön bist du![13]

The music and the poem of this third part are in sharp contrast with the first two sections of the Act III narrative, which are belligerent, denying, in conflict, angry. This advance into serenity fits in with the idea that he is already dead – in a dream state in which we have perceptions contrary to our intentions. And this passage is the summary of his whole life in order to prepare him to cross over into this new land. It is the glory of this act, during which you can experience, in a single time-frame, almost all of what is in the whole piece.

So of course it makes utter sense that he rips his bandages off when he knows she is approaching. He hastens his death because he longs for the moment when he can *really* see her, *really* be one with her – in the state of death. He has already been healed; just knowing she will be here is enough for him to be released.

The final B major chord is the epitome of simplicity after all this agitation, madness, joy and pain. The whole piece is about the fusing of opposites. Everything in the work is about dissonance and harmony, incoherence and absolute understanding. It's like the swirls in the ocean that only seem at a distance to have harmony to them. *Parsifal* is the greatest musical achievement of Wagner, but for emotion and depth of meaning you can't go past *Tristan und Isolde*. This seems to me like a requiem on human love and existence. His next opera would have been about the giving-out of being human.

A lot of people find the role of Tristan to be very complicated and difficult. Actually, it's very straightforward. Trying to 'interpret' this role, in the sense of 'analysing' it, is counterproductive. You have to experience it. And I didn't do that at first. You always have to think technically about this piece, and obviously there are going to be evenings where you're not going to experience the piece because there are technical problems. (I did a performance in Munich when I had been very sick, and I stubbornly was going to get through the piece anyway. I did, but there was no discovery that night.) When it does come together, I'm suddenly and profoundly released.

In that state of release, I experience the added joy of listening to a good colleague. I have been so lucky with the artists with whom I've sung this role. In London I had my own transcendental experience one night singing with Nina Stemme.[14] We were singing the duet together (and I have a darker

---

[13] 'She brings me my final drink. Ah, Isolde, how beautiful you are!'
[14] Born in Stockholm in 1963, Nina Stemme took a vocal course alongside her studies in economics and business management and began to make a name for herself in the early 1990s. Her singing of Isolde at Glyndebourne Festival Opera in 2003 (with Plácido Domingo singing Tristan and Antonio Pappano conducting) attracted much praise. She first sang at Bayreuth in 1994 (Freia in *Das Rheingold*), and has since sung Isolde there on several occasions, beginning in 2005.

voice that kind of suits hers as well), and all of a sudden, I realised that she was trying to match my vibrato. We could almost create one voice in the duet, a function of her generosity and artistry and constant searching for new ways towards beauty. Just like that, for both of us, we're discovering something in this piece. Starting with a technical issue, we were able to hear, feel, experience a totally new thing in this piece.

I've had great Isoldes. My first partner was Iréne Theorin.[15] She'd had much more experience in the role than I, and she helped me so much in my very first Tristan to go beyond just hitting the right notes and getting through it. It was she who started me on the road to, okay, let's explore and see what these two people are going through. And I've sung with the great Evelyn Herlitzius.[16] That woman can't sing the telephone book without interpreting it so brilliantly. And I'm not talking about technical things now – I'm talking about feeling things, experiencing new things that are brought out. Petra Lang[17] brought a unique energy to our collaboration in the Katharina Wagner staging for Bayreuth.

Let's revisit the main themes. Wagner's work is so dense that if you try to think about it too much, you will actually get less out of it, not more. And that is the utility of myth. Jump into this role and realise that you're not performing; you're experiencing it, you're living it yourself.

Then if the audience catches something from that, great. If they don't, then to some degree that's their problem. This is a symphony, and not just of instruments and voices. It's a symphony of souls. No matter what voice sings Tristan, if he can get through it, there will be a different emotion, a different event. That's the whole point of transcending something. That's why, as an audience member, we go to see *Tristan* many different times. We don't go to hear a certain voice or hear it done a certain way; we go to be enlightened, transformed. *Tristan* is about throwing yourself into the insanity of going deeper than anything has ever gone. It really is like adding another dimension to your being. I have the advantage because

---

[15] Iréne Theorin is also a Swedish dramatic soprano born in 1963; her career was launched in Sweden and Denmark. In 2005, in Beijing, she sang Brünnhilde with the Staatstheater Nürnberg in the first-ever performance of *Der Ring des Nibelungen* in China. She first sang Isolde at the Bayreuth Festival in 2008.

[16] Another dramatic soprano born in 1963 (this time in Germany), Evelyn Herlitzius is known especially for her singing of the major roles in Strauss and Wagner. She made her stage debut as Elisabeth in *Tannhäuser* and, as a member of the Semper Oper in Dresden from 1997 to 2000, sang both Elisabeth and Venus in *Tannhäuser*, Sieglinde and Brünnhilde in *Der Ring des Nibelungen* and Kundry in *Parsifal*. She made her Bayreuth debut in 2002, singing Brünnhilde in *Der Ring*, and has since sung Kundry, Ortrud in *Lohengrin* and Isolde there, the last in 2015, in a staging by Katharina Wagner.

[17] Petra Lang (born in Frankfurt am Main in 1962) began her career as a mezzo-soprano, switching to soprano roles in 2012. She began to sing Wagner in the 1994–95 season, appearing as Fricka and Waltraute in a *Ring* cycle in Dortmund, adding Brangäne to her repertoire in Braunschweig in 1995–97. Brangäne was the first role she sang at Bayreuth, in 2005, followed by Ortrud in 2011 and Isolde in 2016.

'Great Isoldes': Iréne Theorin, Evelyn Herlitzius and Petra Lang

I can transform myself. I am a very lucky man. I have the gift – and the good fortune – to be in that position.

As a performer I'm glad that I came to this repertoire, because it does matter. It does matter to let yourself go, and not try to comprehend every little detail of the narrative. Because that's not what being human is about. That's why we have music – because it is a higher form of human communication than the spoken word. The spoken word is just a system of symbols to convey to others ideas we might have. But you can have a certain musical phrase that can elicit a response that, as Tristan says to Marke, is an experience that you cannot otherwise comprehend.

It is a privilege to be able to perform that piece and for a time I thought I might never have the opportunity to do it again. This was the heartbreak of the closure of the theatres at just that time in my career. In February 2020, I was booked to perform *Tristan* in four different productions over the next several seasons. I looked forward to it as a personal opportunity, a further chance to continue a deeply satisfying aesthetic journey. I was at the point with this role that Tristan was an opportunity for self-discovery through sublime music that was just coming out of me. And they were all cancelled. Gone. Vanished. By grace of fortune, I have the opportunity now that I feared I would never have: I will experience the role again.

III
The Ring
of the Nibelung

Loge

A lot of people don't take the role of Loge very seriously. And to be honest neither did I, until I had the chance to perform it. So when the opportunity arose, I wanted to do Loge with an approach that was informed *precisely because* most people don't take him very seriously. The irony is that now, every time I see *Das Rheingold*, I feel that he is the most interesting, and actually the most essential, character in the play to understand.

Remember that Wagner conceived *Das Rheingold* after the other parts of the *Ring* had been thought up; he started with *Siegfried's Death* and went backwards, ending up with *Das Rheingold*. So was his purpose to lighten up the heaviness of the *Ring*, or to write an expository introduction to it? I don't think those considerations had anything to do with it. He was writing to show the gods at a different time in their lives – a time when they committed the great sins of their youth.

When the action of this play takes place, we're seeing how young Wotan became the Wotan who did the great and tragic acts of the saga. This is a family of young gods that have the talent and ability to be the great politicians of the universe, but they don't have the wisdom and self-understanding to do it – as we will see, to the ultimate shame of the universe.

Wotan's problem is precisely that he's a *young* god. He's powerful, but he's not all-powerful. His power comes from the law, the runes, the agreements, the legislation that has been literally etched into the staff of his spear. But it becomes too much – he can't control it; rather, it comes to control and limit him. All that comes later. When we meet him in *Rheingold*, we meet the young gods, the gods who are more emotional and petulant, like Thor and his hammer, prone to anger. Or pure, virginal sexuality in Freia. They eat her apples. It's a somewhat incestuous, self-perpetuating thing. So there's a lot of fun to be had in *Rheingold* because we see all of the gods having difficulty with what really are pretty petty problems – at least compared to what comes later, which are existential problems.

You've got a young Wotan trying to decide whether he is Licht or Schwarz. If you consider only how they behave in *Rheingold*, there's little difference between him and Alberich: they both are the elite, and they both want complete control over everything. They both make stupid decisions and funny things happen to both of them. The mere idea of Wotan agreeing to give Freia away to have his castle built, with the unspoken intention that he'll figure out a way to get out of it when the time comes… I mean, c'mon! The rest are no more mature. Freia is supposed to be an Aphrodite character, but she behaves exactly like a dumb blonde and no more. And Fricka is the Real Housewife of Valhalla. I can see why people experience *Rheingold* as light and frothy.

But it's a very important prelude, because it shows the gods before they were really corrupted. It shows Wotan before the curse. And it shows that he had foreknowledge: we see that Loge expressly told him, don't do this. Loge's purpose is to be the *consigliere* for the godfather, the *Dramaturg* for the *regisseur*. What happens is that Wotan – like any politician – will say to Loge, I'm going to do this. Find a way for me to do it. Legal or not, give me the justification. And that's what Loge does.

Loge doesn't like being in that position. He may be a trickster, he may be sly, he may even be funny, but he's an extraordinarily dangerous entity. He comes off very spontaneous, but behind him is true power – elemental power – and he's a dangerous being.

Wagner stitched together the character of Loge between Loki, the Norse god of mischief and trickery, and Loge, the god of fire, adding certain attributes like the mythological King Midas, who possessed the touch of gold. So you put these characters together to create what I like to call an 'elemental'. Loge is a demi-god, according to Wagner – part god, part element of fire. He is like Shiva, who both destroys and creates. That is what makes Loge so interesting. He is the character that drives the entire action of *Rheingold*. And in some ways, he is a distillation of the entire *Ring* cycle in one being. Creation, destruction, recreation, renewed destruction, the cycle goes on.

Loge freely acknowledges this dual existence as god and as element, and we see him in both states. He says at the end of *Rheingold*, do I want to stay sentient? Do I want to remain this quick, intelligent, decisive form that acts like a god, or do I want to return to my elemental form, a force that will quench and never be quenched? It seems that he chooses the latter. At the end of *Walküre*, Loge returns, but not as a character. Rather he is summoned by Wotan to appear as the element of fire. It seems that, in the intervening period, Loge has made his decision: 'Nah. I have spent my time in Valhalla, I have been the advisor to Wotan, and he's not listened to anything I've said'.

I remember a performance by Siegfried Jerusalem, at the Metropolitan Opera, in the Otto Schenk[1] production. When Jerusalem came out as Loge,

---

[1] The Viennese Otto Schenk (b. 1930) is an actor and a director in both theatre and opera. His naturalist production of *Der Ring des Nibelungen* at the Metropolitan Opera in New York in 1986 was hailed by traditionalists as being true to Wagner's vision; it remained in repertoire at the Met for over twenty years.

he sang it, and I absolutely adopt that approach. I believe that Wagner intended this role to be sung by a Heldentenor, not a character tenor. He didn't want the voice to be made crazy or crackly or whatever; he wanted it to be sung just like you would sing Lohengrin or Siegmund. And Jerusalem, when he provoked Alberich to turn into a frog (or salamander, I like to think), there's this look between him and Wotan, and they both laugh. Then Wotan passes in front of Jerusalem, congratulating himself, and as he passes, Jerusalem's face changes and turns to pure hatred for Wotan. In that moment I understood what Loge was doing.

Loge despises the way he is treated. No one speaks well of him. No one is fond of him or respects him, or is even kind to him. And yet when he has his *arioso* about the power of the love of women, even the gods themselves are caught up by its beauty, wisdom and truth.

Loge is, in a sense, a manipulative puppet-master. But he's not doing it out of an evil design. He's doing it because it is what he is – he is elemental. You notice that Wotan always calls him, summons him to appear and perform upon command. To Loge it feels like he's a servant or a pet, like 'Come here, boy, come here, boy'.

In his first scene with the gods, Loge behaves like a stereotypical sleazy lawyer. Wotan says you promised to get me out of this and Loge says no, I only promised to try, which irritates the hell out of everybody else on stage. He then goes on to say that there is no way out because there is no substitute for a woman's love, and if that is what Fasolt expects, then that is what Fasolt will insist upon. Fafner, Loge need not say, is another matter entirely. Loge notes that there is always the power of the gold. Wotan asks how that might be obtained, and Loge says by theft.

Keep in mind that those two words, 'by theft', are marked *marcato sforzando*, with the additional marking 'very bitter'. When I performed it (as a lawyer with a hat and suit and glasses, but also a giant red cape) and I got to that part, Loge finally turns on Wotan and says, in effect, what are you trying to get me to tell you? There is only one way for you to do this. There has always been only one way for you to do this – to get the giants to build this castle for you, to get the power of the ring – there is only one way: through theft. Through force. Through fascism. And this is the moment when Wotan realises that he is going to do it. One of the great moments of the *Ring* – Wotan's original sin. And even though Wotan succeeds in the theft, and Loge helps him to succeed – by brutally disfiguring Alberich, cutting off his hand along with the ring – Loge warns Wotan to get rid of it.

Loge takes the curse very seriously. Loge says to Alberich, go your merry way, be free, and he hears Alberich ask of himself – and of Wotan, and by extension of Loge himself – are you free? Are you really free? And, of course, the answer is no. They are not, and never will be, free ever again.

I find Loge to be the most interesting character to play in the entire *Ring*. Loge can always win the day because he tells people what they want to hear. He plays to their egos, and that's what happens with Alberich. Oh, that's really impressive, that you can get that big, you are so clever. He easily fools Wotan, Alberich, the Giants. It takes little to imagine that he was the negotiator between Wotan and the Giants, that he saw Fasolt become enamoured of Freia, that he used that to cut the deal, that he was prepared to alter it down the line as need required. How can a god or a demigod deal with a duplicitous elemental like Loge? You can't. Loge will always find a way.

Mind you, it doesn't work out well for him in the end, does it? Loge remains in thrall to Wotan, even in his elemental form. At the end of *Walküre*, when Wotan summons him, he has to appear. And, most movingly, in Waltraute's monologue in Act I of *Götterdämmerung*, we are given an image of Loge chained to the table, captured, unable to leave, and vulnerable to Wotan's power. Wotan will stab him in the chest, emitting fire and rendering all of the gods to ash – Loge included, presumably. So it seems like the agency and the options that Loge talks about at the end of *Rheingold* – will I stay or won't I, what should I do – seem to be illusory, and his status remains as a servant, or even slave.

But the point is that, as the gods diminish to nothing, to an irrelevance, they end in pure fire – Loge's fire. Fire is a symbol of purification, as it is in the forging of Siegfried's sword – what can't be welded has to be completely destroyed, melted, purified and re-forged. So one could think of the character of Loge, posing the questions at the end of *Rheingold*, as unchained, loosened and converted to his pure elemental self. As a sentient being, Loge ends with the gods; as a pure element, he persists. After *Rheingold*, we hear his presence in the orchestra only as fire, never as a character who speaks to others or engages with other characters.

It's also clever, and within the theatrical tradition of the 'aside', that Wagner invites Loge to have a direct relationship with the audience that is in many ways more informed than his relationship with the other onstage characters. Characters addressing the audience, including them by commenting on the stage action, is a centuries-old dramaturgical practice. For example, in the letter scene in *Twelfth Night*, Sebastian watches Malvolio be tricked and then turns and tells the audience that, if he saw this played on a stage, he would 'condemn it as an improbable farce'. So, here, the other characters in *Rheingold* think Loge an idiot, dismissible. But the audience knows him as the only character in the *Ring* who breaks the fourth wall and invites them

Loge

in. He not only addresses the audience; he asks their advice. Loge invites the audience to contextualise what is happening.

From a vocal point of view, it is the lowest of the tenor roles. It has a high G in it, and that's it. It was made for the Heldentenor voice and it's extraordinarily enjoyable to play as a character. Loge was the last of the *Ring* roles that I performed. I had to beg the leadership at the New National Theatre in Tokyo, to include Loge in my *Ring* assignments when they were remounting the Helsinki Götz Friedrich[2] production. It was such a joy, because it helps you to understand the characters, going from Loge to Siegmund.

---

[2] A hugely influential director of opera and theatre, Götz Friedrich (1930-2000) first studied with Walter Felsenstein at the Komische Oper in East Berlin. His first major production, a provocative *Tannhäuser* at Bayreuth in 1972, attracted much controversy; in Stockholm later that year, for a production of Janáček's *Jenůfa*, he defected to the west. Thereafter he was principal director at the Hamburg State Opera (1972-81) and director of productions at the Royal Opera House, Covent Garden (1977-81), where he had already (1973-77) staged his first *Ring* Cycle; thereafter he joined the Deutsche Oper Berlin, where he remained until his death. Although he worked across the operatic repertoire, he was especially known for his stagings of Wagner. His last full *Ring* cycle dated from 1996 and was restaged at the Finnish National Opera in Helsinki in 2000 and revived in 2004.

Siegmund

Now for Siegmund, a pretty tortured character. To my mind, he is the only classic hero in Wagner. I understand a hero, a *Held*, to be someone who engages with the ultimate at stake, knowing he will fail, but doing it anyway. The accepted image of the 'hero' is easier, and more Disney-like: the guy who rushes in to save the damsel from distress. And yes, they do that sometimes. But the 'hero' I refer to takes a journey that is the consequence of a more internal struggle than with outward forces like dragons and thorn bushes. The true hero fights a losing battle and persists in doing so even after he understands the futility of the fight. It is a tale of obstinacy that is presented as heroic because it reaffirms some central conviction of being a human being.

Siegmund is doomed from the very beginning. He wears it like a shirt. He discusses it in detail. He is Wehwalt, the bearer of sorrow. Think about it. He grows up with Wälse, but at the highest moment of need he spends all his time with his father until he is abandoned. He has no social skills, no experience of love. Upon being abandoned, he finds his mother has been killed and his sister violently absconded with. He spends years trying to acclimate himself to other clans, and is spectacularly unsuccessful. He is driven off. He eventually finds his only experience of love through an incestuous relationship with his own sister. The sword he was promised converts from an instrument of vindication to one of betrayal. And why? Because Fricka doesn't like him. Because the gods, fate, the tides of eventuality, have him on the short list of the utterly doomed. He is a complete tragic character, Sisyphus. He is the only one in the *Ring* who succeeds by persisting though in a state of preordained failure.

Mind you, in emphasising his failure, I emphasise his irony. Wotan sired him for one purpose – to obtain the ring from Fafner. He was supposed to succeed. And yet, as things turn out, he never gets anywhere close to what he was meant to accomplish. His greatest failure was to fail to live long enough to do the one thing he was born to do. By comparison, Siegfried is an entirely different kind of hero: without fear, without knowledge of his past, without even a sense of morality or love. And he's the one who gets the ring. Siegfried lacks any of the understanding of the world, or of the evils of the world, that Siegmund possesses.

Performing Siegmund is something of a challenge, but for unorthodox reasons. It's probably the most famous music of the entire *Ring*. Certainly, some of the most beautiful music in the *Ring*. And therefore, if you want to do this role, you must accept an extra-musical, extra-theatrical concern: you do this in public and you will be compared to every artist who has sung it in the history of the universe. So it's a challenge in that sense, but not in a lot of others. The length of the role is a walk in the park. And it's not a high role either. (It's interesting how they progress, that Loge is low, Siegmund is a little higher, Siegfried in *Siegfried* is up there and the tessitura of the *Götterdämmerung* Siegfried is just unfair.)

The role also invites lapses of taste in the *Wälse* cries in Act I of *Die Walküre*. In the early twentieth-century, people did make a meal of it, and it seems a little silly perhaps to us because it seems like the star tenor is holding up the show to demonstrate how long he can hold a G natural. These days the person responsible for the musical quality of the performance – the conductor – has rather more influence than when Melchior[1] would arrive in Kansas City in the morning train, sing Siegmund and move on to Indianapolis the next day. It took quite a long time for the tradition to build, and some of the recordings we have are from tenors who were a bit ticked off.[2] Lucky for me, I don't hold these notes forever because, frankly, I can't. The only important thing is that the second one needs to be more emphatic. Which probably means it needs to be a little longer. But just a little. And ideally you should try to *crescendo* a bit on each of them. The point is to get to '*Wo ist dein Schwert?*'[3] I mean, that is what he's singing about, isn't it?

I don't find the role challenging musically or dramatically. A high baritone could sing the entire role of Siegmund, particularly Act II. I think the greatest challenge of the role is to personify the very core of it – fighting against fate. It is the brief story of a tragic hero.

Why do people enter the OK Corral, or meet the train at High Noon, knowing the odds are against them? Because they must, somehow. Siegmund is incapable of doing otherwise. You have to be careful in the Act I narrative not to make him seem whiney – not to turn him into a pitiable shmoo, asking Sieglinde to become his Agony Auntie (this is what they did to me, why are they so mean, why do I always end up getting

---

[1] The Danish tenor Lauritz Melchior (1890–1973), whose international career began with his engagement to sing Siegmund and Parsifal for the re-opening of the festival in Bayreuth in 1924.
[2] A chain of historical recordings of 'Wälse! Wälse' (with the subtitle 'old school tenors') can be found on YouTube at https://www.youtube.com/watch?v=0JS0lVlaK08.
[3] 'Where is your sword?'

thrown out of town). The danger is making him pathetic. Siegmund is not pathetic; he is a true hero on the hero's short journey to death.

The best way to approach it, it seems to me, is that he just didn't know about the world that eventually defeats him. The only thing he knows of nobility are the hunts and the fights with his father Wotan at his side. The only thing he knows of chivalry is nothing. Look at his behaviour in the *Todesverkündigung*.[4] He asks questions and, when he gets an answer he doesn't like, he just turns his back on Brünnhilde. No negotiation, no discussion. Just no. His response to learning that Sieglinde bears a child is to say with no hesitation that he will kill both of them rather than journey to Valhalla alone. He believes that there can only be existence with them together, and he will harbour no other possibility. This is stern, irrational heroism – bold action in the face of doom. Like the great heroes, the quest costs Siegmund his life.

The role of Siegmund is not nuanced or subtle. But before leaving him, we should throw in here the concept of sacrifice. The gods never sacrificed anything; history for them is a series of transactions. Looked at this way, one can question whether the gods are 'heroic' in the way we've been discussing. Siegmund's very fibre is shown in Act II, when he is prepared to sacrifice himself, his sister, and all that he has, in testimony to his and Sieglinde's love for each other. This concept of intentional sacrifice of self is one that, of course, is the final gesture of the *Ring*, and the entire topic of *Parsifal*.

---

[4] Annunciation of death, in Act II.

Siegfried in *Siegfried*

There are easier entrances in opera than coming on with a bear. I'm not absolutely sure what Wagner was hoping to accomplish with it, and I have to hope there were easier ways to accomplish it. But I think it's to show the childish nature, the playful *persona* of Siegfried. And also the fact that Siegfried can be – not brutal – but aggressive. He's learned everything from the forest, from the wild. It's more of a challenge to the audience to watch a bear than to me to act with one. I've done it with a dancer in a bear suit that I'm holding on to. I've seen it with a projection of a bear in the doorway, which scares Mime. But it's kind of fun and no harm done.

Technically it's a difficult entrance – it's almost impossible to sing, triplets in a tempo marked '*rasch*' (quick), going up to a high C, which I don't have, and neither do most tenors. So it comes out as a *Jubelschrei*, a cry of jubilation. Tradition has it that if you don't sing it and hold it, you're not a good tenor.

Let's pause right here. I like to assume that Wagner wanted things sung the way he wrote them. And it's a good general rule that, once you're tried everything else, you can always sing it as the composer actually wrote it and see how that comes out. Here, and in a similar passage at the end of the Rhinemaidens' scene in *Götterdämmerung* Act III, he wrote it straight. He didn't write a fermata on that high C. 'Hoi-ho' sings the chorus; 'hoi-ho, hoi-he' sings Siegfried in response. Not 'hoi-ho, hoi – go out for a Starbucks latte and return to the theatre – he.' Same thing at the end of Act II Scene 4, '*meinem frohen Muthe…*'. It's not even meant to be sung – it's a semiquaver that you touch on, on the way to the next one, part of a sung phrase, not a series of singular and independent notes. It has almost the same effect as a grace-note in performance at tempo. But these things happen.

Back to Siegfried's entrance. Problematic as it is for the performer, it entirely succeeds for the audience. It establishes, first, that things that scare Mime don't scare Siegfried – as we know, a critical fact. And it also establishes that all of Siegfried's learning has come directly from the natural world, not through man-made laws or customs – as we know, another crucial fact. So once again, hats off to Wagner the dramatist.

Let's also be clear that living without fear doesn't mean he is insensate. Does Siegfried learn anything cautionary, growing up in the woods? Of course he does. But he doesn't fear death. He has no well-developed sense of what not having life means. He's seen animals die but that's about it – he's observed it. He has no sense of anything after this existence. With that open attitude there's nothing about death to fear. It doesn't mean, either, that if a dragon attacks him, he's not going to jump out of the way. Of course he is. But for him it's a way of going about one's life, almost a game – though he doesn't know what the rules are or what the goal is. Indeed, it is Siegfried's acquiring these insights that is much of the action in the piece.

The role is a huge challenge in stamina and technique, but not in terms of drama. In terms of dramatic action, all Siegfried does is respond to what's happening around him – until the very end, that is, as we'll discuss. The challenge for me was just to physically learn the piece and put it into your body and make it yours and have the stamina to do it. I had been singing a lot of Tannhäuser, Lohengrin and Parsifal. I was well underway. Erik in *Fliegende Hollander*. The more lyrical side of Wagner. I had not attacked, other than the first act of *Walküre* in concert, what it meant to perform the *Ring*. I had not learned yet that there is a different way you must sing in the *Ring*. Others may differ with me, but I have experienced it to be so. It's an entirely distinctive type of theatre, calling for an entirely distinctive manner of performing. And it was intentionally so.

This was Wagner's new art that he was bringing to the stage, where the text is as important as the music. And it's all through-composed, without the light sung recitative to advance the story and then, separately, the aria to express inner emotion. He had written that kind of theatre and he was not interested in that anymore. He had been experimenting with that before the *Ring* but now he wanted to make his complete work, his signature work, a new kind of work entirely. People may forget, or perhaps not give due emphasis to, the fact that he intentionally wanted to create a new art, distinct from the lyrical art of the musical stage. This vision had never been attempted, much less accomplished, before. And although Wagner intended that the Italian lyrical vocal tradition would continue to sing in his work, he realised that he was asking of his singer an approach to the text that was entirely new.

For instance, take this opening scene of *Siegfried*. I didn't realise this until we started actually doing it, but it's in that scene that you have an actual character tenor onstage alongside you. These were big, strong, powerful tenors, capable of bringing vivid life to a role through the text. They were powerful voices, and in the old days many character tenors developed into Heldentenors.

So here I am, I've learned the words and the notes and I look around and I found myself onstage with probably one of the best of our time, Gerhard Siegel, as Mime.[5] Gerhard had already sung Siegfried in smaller houses. And he understood the approach, the technique, of what amounted to performing recitative with a full orchestra under you. So, you can't use a full tone, as you would in an aria with a long line. You have to open the voice more, make it brighter, make the text more forward, place the sound itself behind the teeth, like biting an apple. In *Tannhäuser* I still had that Italianate line. That was what I was used to using for years, and to some successful effect. And then all of a sudden, I was confronted with the reality that, okay, I spent two years studying these two roles, I get onstage – in Bayreuth, of all places – and I suddenly realise that I have the wrong technique for this role.

My coaches and I had decided that I would wait until my late forties for Siegfried, but then the opportunity came – Bayreuth wanted me to do Siegfried after I had jumped in as Tannhäuser there for a season. I talked to my voice teacher, and he said, you're in your early forties, the timing is okay, you just need enough time to learn the role. But we both didn't realise that I had absolutely no experience with this absolutely new art form. So, when I got onstage, it was actually Gerhard Siegel who helped me – not only technically with what I had to do, but dramatically, finding out what kind of character I had to portray. That characterisation, it turned out, was compelled by the way you had to produce the sound for it.

When you're fighting this text all the time, you've got two strong character tenors going after each other. And if you're not careful, Siegfried can come off as brutal, a bully, almost fascist. He could also come off as ignorant or dumb, a Baby Huey.[6] Neither of those is helpful to advancing the story that Wagner wrote. You can make him come off as a *Riesen-Baby*, a giant child. Many of us who do the role have weight problems or can look innocent or doughy onstage. There is a way to play it as innocent, but not dumb – large but not bumping into walls. Even the music can make Siegfried come off as an extremely unsympathetic character. I had to learn on the fly, very quickly.

It's hard to play a nature child. To play less is the key to young Siegfried. The less you intend, and the more you allow the music and text to guide you, the better off you are. You can't allow brutality to creep in, or Baby Huey or sentimental dumbness. Because there are no actual people that

---

[5] Gerhard Siegel (b. 1963) made his Covent Garden debut as Mime in 2004 and sang the role at Bayreuth from 2006 to 2008, making it his signature role. He has also sung Loge, Lohengrin, Parsifal and Tristan.
[6] An American cartoon character in the form of a huge duckling, dim-witted, naïve and clumsy. He made his first appearance in 1950.

grow up in the jungle without human contact, there's no model for that extreme. But to play it somewhere in the middle – someone without fear, without guile, acting naturally without being destructive. He's seen sex and procreation. He knows what happens. He sees that mothers care for their little foxes and bring them food and care for them while they're young. He realises that they are helpless, but he doesn't sentimentalise it.

(The only time Siegfried should come off as unsympathetic is Act II and thereafter in *Götterdämmerung*. Why? Because his drinking the potion and forgetting about Brünnhilde can explain a lot of things, but it cannot explain why he becomes a liar, dishonest, a manipulator. These are things he does on his own, without the help of the elixir. But we'll deal with that whole character arc later.[7])

Siegfried threatens physical violence on Mime, and that's hard for audiences to accept from a hero. But remember that Mime raised Siegfried for non-altruistic reasons. So we don't know what traumas Siegfried has been put through. He expressly says to Mime: 'I hate you'. I have found that the key might be, just play him as a teenager. He is impetuous, he is searching, and there are moments of grabbing and shaking and threatening and breaking things. But I don't think he would actually be violent – at least in Act I. He has learned a lot of bad things from Mime but I don't think he would hurt him. He has learned that strength and coercion are what get some things done. He wouldn't harm him, though, until that moment in Act II – and he immediately regrets it. 'Now I am alone.' But at that moment he says that a custom, a duty, a *Zoll*, must be paid in order for him to move to the next stage of his life. 'My only company in the world was a horrible, hateful dwarf who wanted to kill me. I was strong enough.'

This day would have been like every other day in Siegfried's life, except that he has what appears at first to be an innocent question: Why does he look different from Mime? Isn't that what starts the story? All other animal pairs and packs look like each other, but he and Mime don't. And the entire narrative stems from posing that question. Siegfried asks who were his father and mother, and when Mime says he was both, Siegfried sees it's a lie. It's the persistence of that inquiry that causes the action: This is Sieglinde, this is the sword, now I have a mission, I'm going to get out of here. He is at the moment in his life where it's time for him to leave Mime, but he doesn't have the knowledge or skill he needs – he needs a sword and a destiny.

---

[7] On pp. 68–76, below.

Siegfried in Siegfried

Why does he need a sword? We'll never know. But we do know that he has needed one for a long time. Mime has been trying to make a sword that will hold up to Siegfried's might.

Indeed, on this very day, Siegfried's been out in the forest waiting, expecting a new sword to be made. That's why he first comes in – to test the most recently forged sword. Siegfried's frustration has been building for a long time. How many times has Mime failed? Twenty? I think the sword represents Siegfried's attaining maturity and having the sword triggers his need to go out on the hero's quest.

That's why Wotan shows up mysteriously at this very point – at the time that Siegfried is about to gain his sword and leave. Nor is this sword to be repaired – it is first to be destroyed.

The allegory of the sword is that, once shattered or cracked or broken, the object is irretrievably lost, cannot be made whole. It's the story of the phoenix: completely destroy it and then renew it from its own ashes. It has to be an entirely new sword, and Siegfried is the only one who intuitively knows this. Out of complete innocence, Siegfried knows that you can't take your father's broken sword and fix it. It has to be his own sword. Once Siegfried has reformed the sword with his own might, Wotan has no further lineage in it and can no longer help him. The sword is an emblem both of Siegfried's independent, unbridled agency, and of the end of Wotan's interventions. Wotan now has been rendered without influence, because it's Siegfried's sword now, not the one that Wotan gave his father. The sword has been transformed and now is a tool of man, not the gods.

This is made transparently obvious in Act III when Wotan and Siegfried meet. In *Walküre* Act II, Wotan's spear shaft breaks the sword forged by the gods. In *Siegfried* Act III, Wotan's spear shaft shatters when it encounters the sword forged by men.

Upon Siegfried's return – after the Wanderer scene, coming back in the hope of having his father's sword – he is clearly manipulated by Mime to visit *Neidhöhle*, the cave of envy, and kill Fafner. Why does Siegfried agree to do this? He's intrigued by this idea of fear. He still hasn't feared death, and this sounds exciting. He's sad that his mother died but it doesn't provoke anxiety or fear, which Mime presents as an entirely distinctive attribute, or experience. For Siegfried everything is discovery – I'd like to learn that. He doesn't know love or hatred (as opposed to aggression). Like any teenager, he wants to learn who his father and mother were and what is this thing Mime calls fear.

In Act II, he takes very little action on his own initiative until he hears and understands the Woodbird. Think about it: he walks into the forest, tells Mime to go away, ruminates on his circumstances, is threatened by and kills the dragon – all these scenes are either without dramatic action or in response to action that is initiated by someone else. And again it is a lesson for the performer – the simpler you keep this, the better off you are in the character.

What I have started thinking about in later performances is the Woodbird – we think of her as the helpful influence on Siegfried, guiding, assisting. But is she? After killing the dragon, Siegfried is ready to go on with his life, but the Woodbird tells him that he should go in and get two things: the Tarnhelm and the ring. Why? The ring is cursed and will destroy everyone who possesses it. Why does she direct him to the curse? Loge warned Wotan: don't wear that thing as a token of your power. The moment Wotan puts it on, that's the beginning of the fall of the gods. Harry Kupfer[8] staged that dialogue between the Woodbird and Siegfried as Wotan manipulating what the Woodbird says to him. Maybe so. But that's not consistent with the fact that the Woodbird is eventually chased away by Wotan's ravens, which implies that Wotan wants her gone. Anyway, I got to thinking about that, and I'd like to think that the Woodbird may have assumed, because Siegfried's so innocent and pure, that the ring somehow wouldn't hurt him. But think – if Mime had come back before the Woodbird instructed Siegfried, Mime could have just walked into the cave and taken the ring. So might Alberich have, or even Wotan. But once Siegfried has the ring on his finger, Mime has to kill him because he knows that, unless by force, he will never get the ring.

That, too, leads to why Siegfried can suddenly hear Mime's thoughts. This is worth noting, really an astonishing piece of dramaturgy. This is pre-Freud. Until Ibsen and Chekhov and O'Neill, you don't have plays about people who have a subconscious life of which even they may be unaware, but that the audience can read. It's a remarkably prescient scene, relying as it does on the assumption that what people say, and what they are subconsciously thinking, are two different things. This is Stanislavsky – Siegfried and the audience can hear not only what Mime says, but also what Mime chooses not to say. For Siegfried, it is simply astonishing. When Siegfried first hears that Mime intends to do him harm, it's almost amusing in its audacity. 'Like, really? You think you can do that?'

---

[8] Harry Kupfer (1935–2019) studied in East Germany, not least with Walter Felsenstein, making his career there before being invited, in 1978, to direct *Der fliegende Holländer* at Bayreuth, staging it as originating in Senta's imagination. His 1988 Bayreuth *Ring* initially received a pasting from the critics, though it now has many admirers. He took up the post of chief director at the Komische Oper Berlin in 1981, his last production there being Britten's *The Turn of the Screw* in 2002.

Siegfried in Siegfried

Keep in mind, too, that Wagner himself changed his emphasis, in terms of the moral tale, away from Siegfried and more to Brünnhilde. As his own ideas developed, it became not so much that Siegfried, light of the world, offspring of the Wälsungs, *Erlöser* (saviour) of the human condition, would vindicate the destiny of man, but rather that Brünnhilde would, through love and sacrifice. So again, as far as the role of Siegfried goes, the less you play it, the more naïve you remain, the closer you remain to the central current that runs through it.

Then we have the confrontation between Wotan and Siegfried. In this scene the old world ends and the new one begins. The future is not guided by law, expressed in enforceable runes written on a spear shaft, but instead by anarchic human impetuosity. But again, that's for the philosopher in the audience. For the performer onstage, much less is at stake. At this moment he has only one goal on his mind, and he's being distracted from it. Wotan is in his way – get out of my way. At first he's kind of friendly; the Wanderer wants to hear his story and Siegfried is glad to tell it. The rudeness that Siegfried expresses to Wotan doesn't arise until he feels he's being mocked by this old man.

And then it develops to the point that Wotan says: 'I will stand in your way'. Once starting to get irked, Siegfried asks him about his eye in a sort of mocking way. Siegfried thinks he's being laughed at and he'll have none of it. 'I see that you lost an eye. That must have been from someone who got super-irritated with you because of your stupid questions and the way you block peoples' path. Get out of the way or I'll knock out the other one.' Wanderer starts saying things that make Siegfried uncomfortable: 'Since before you were born I loved you. When you were in the womb I knew you'. This is something Siegfried has been looking for: he seeks to learn not only what is fear, but also what is love. And when he hears that from Wotan – 'I have cherished you and all your kind, so please don't awaken my anger because it will destroy both of us' – that's when Siegfried decides this guy is in the way. Wotan then allows Siegfried to see the fire on the *Fels*, the rock or mountain. Loge flares up at that moment because Wotan wills for Siegfried to see it. And, of course, it is at that moment that Wotan intentionally forces the issue: having held out the fire as a temptation, Wotan says *Zurück!* Go back from this flame. And the teenage Siegfried predictably and understandably says *Zurück* yourself, you stupid man. I have to go up there. I've been told that's where I will find my bride.

It's as if Wotan is saying, Disobey me. I have promised my most precious child, who disobeyed me, to one who I insist will now disobey me in turn. Only by that great disobedience does Siegfried gain the right – the moral universal right – to gain the love of Brünnhilde.

Then we have the great final scene. Wagner, in his infinite wisdom, has chosen, after an extremely long period of recitative, where you are spitting your words out like a machine gun, followed by power moments like the Forging Scene, followed by incredibly lyric moments in Act II with big outbursts, to place the performer in a final scene where magnificent huge *legato* lines have to be poured out in close conjunction with a soprano who is absolutely fresh. So technically it's the most challenging part of the role, and the tenor has to just get through it. You know you're having a good night when you can get these gorgeous lines out. '*Sangs't du mir nicht, dein Wissen sei…*'[9] is almost Otello. It's a giant dramatic Italian melodic line. And it's just the two of you, going back and forth the entire duet. You almost never sing together.

So technically that is the hardest thing about the end. You have to learn through many performances over many years how to pace yourself in each of the previous acts so that each of those three acts can achieve the best effect that they can.

Once we get to this point, the fact that he discovers fear – '*Das ist kein Mann*'[10] – is not to be confused with his being scared. Rather, he's not sure what to do. For Siegfried, the decisive attribute of fear is not being scared – it's loss of control, the state of not knowing what next to do. He knows that if he gets bitten by a snake he may die, but it doesn't provoke fear because he's not scared of death. He sees death and understands it as separation from something he'd like to know more about. And he's killed for food. But he hasn't killed within society. He regrets killing Fafner because that animal could speak. The fear that Siegfried discovers through Brünnhilde is finding himself within the unknown – that he's not in control anymore.

Listen to him. He says, why are my hands shaking? Why is my breath shallow? Why is my heart beating out of my chest? Why do I not know what to do? Why do I feel like running away at the same time I feel like waking her up? What are these things I have never experienced? Indeed, he says, why am I a coward? In other words, why do I not know what to do, instinctively? He knew what to do with the dragon, with Mime. He has had a direct approach to everything. Not now. He even knows that his own body is not in his control anymore. Is this fear? My wife has taught me what fear is. Uncertainty is what fear is for him. And he sings it with joy: she taught me what fear is! How do I retrieve my power and strength? I have to wake up the woman.

But he stops: how sweet her lips are! He begins to experience – again, for the first time in his life – what it is like to have a wife, a partner, the

[9] 'Did you not sing to me that your knowledge….'
[10] 'This is no man.'

matching opposite to him. And he sees how beautiful and how different this is, compared to what he's experienced before. He keeps trying to touch her – she's breathing, her breast is rising, her lips are so soft. How do I wake her? He starts yelling at her: Wake up! Wake up! She doesn't hear him of course. He says: 'I'm going to suck out from the lips this sweet life, even though it may kill me'. As if he had sucked out snake poison from his arm, that the natural gesture is to suckle life itself.

There's something elemental in this kiss. It's like hoping for a reaction, a response. The one thing I learned not to do is to look at that moment as Prince Charming and Sleeping Beauty. Siegfried doesn't know how to kiss. Clumsy is great in staging this moment. It speaks of elemental need, not romance.

After that, once she asks where the hero is who awakened me, from this point on all Siegfried wants is sexual consummation. He doesn't even know that's what it is – he doesn't have any basis to understand, much less empathise, that she would be constrained by social mores or have any objection to it. He's seen it in the woods. It's the natural order of things. He's sexually urgent from that time on. Once uncertainty – that is, fear – is overcome, it is replaced by pressing sexual alertness. Now his destiny has been kept, this is his wife, this is what is supposed to happen and all he knows now is to do. The rest of the scene is easy to play – Siegfried understands what's happening and it's Brünnhilde who knows fear now. The whole rest of the scene is *'sei mein'*. He's trying to talk her into bed. Arousal is a natural thing. She's terrified of not having her powers, not being a god. Indeed, what Wotan threatened her with is being in sexual thrall to a man. And this is it. You'd have to interview a Brünnhilde on this part of it, but from Siegfried's perspective it's not helpful to assume that he is capable of sympathising with her plight.

Siegfried is such a natural child that he has one small narrative running through the entire piece, and that is his story. From the outside we watch him and say is he brutal, does he learn fear, what kind of fear. I have to decide that as a performer, but once I've decided that, that's it. I cannot care about fear or Mime or the dragon. I have to care only about my thread of the narrative. It keeps it simple and direct to the character's purpose. It is up to Siegfried to make this story even happen. All the other characters are the more interesting because they are more complex. Siegfried is not complex. At least not in this piece.

In *Götterdämmerung*, on the other hand....

Siegfried in *Götterdämmerung*

There are few delights in music like the opening of *Siegfried* Act III, when we are introduced to an entirely heightened brand of music-making, announcing Wagner's achievement as a masterful, innovative composer. Nor, either, is there much to match that prophetic E flat minor chord that opens *Götterdämmerung*. The Norns have been weaving their web – threads of connection between time and space. The Norns don't control fate; they spin it, memorialise it, and make sure it stays orderly. In Wagner's music it seems like they're spinning a web, a network of interconnections, rather than a linear travel through time and space. And the protagonists of the epic, whether the gods or dwarfs or the new race of man, seem to be caught in this new web of fate.

The role of Siegfried in *Götterdämmerung* is confusing and deeply flawed in its construction. We know that Wagner changed his mind about the importance of the role of Siegfried in the moral narrative of the *Ring*. And the Norns scene helps to understand Siegfried's change of personality, his change of character. Siegfried's almost a non-*Held*, a non-hero, in this piece, because you cannot follow the action of the play without seeing his flaws. And these are flaws that are not caused by fate; they are caused by his own actions, the consequences of his own choices.

I've performed the role over 70 times, but I have to say that this is a character that I still don't fully understand. The role is much easier to sing than the young Siegfried. But trying to have it make sense is very much more difficult.

Nor am I alone. I've had a lot of good directors, but even these directors have had to jump over the complexities and inconsistencies in some of the scenes, because there's just no way to play it with strict dramatic narrative integrity. I've even had some people say that, in the '*Falsche Gunther*' scene that ends Act I, I just don't know what to do with it.

It seems important, and helpful, to observe that, in many ways, *Götterdämmerung* is not a tragedy but rather a melodrama. It has heightened stakes that don't arise from the demands of the action or of the character within the action; they arise from the choice of the author. The entire Third Act, though most interesting to sing, makes little sense in terms of plot –

Siegfried in Götterdämmerung

it's a set-up just for the purpose of his being killed by Hagen. The other characters are well thought-out to carry forth Wagner's plan. But when he changed from Siegfried's being the ultimate *Erlöser* to Brünnhilde's having that responsibility, he didn't know what to do with the character.

We have to ask the question at the very beginning of this piece, what has been the relationship between these two? It certainly isn't love in the sense of self-sacrifice. Neither one of them comes across as devoted to each other, for whatever reason. Even at Act III we're starting to get a little Tristan – is it possible to have love in any state but death?

I can do the role. And as so many Wagner roles, for the first dozen or so performances my first concern was how to get through this. But later, working on it from a place of relative confidence, and examining what happens in the play, I'm not sure it's possible to find an acceptable level of narrative consistency. I've made choices, but they are not compelled by reason or deduction. It's like *Lear* – the narrative is fundamentally flawed.

At the outset, Siegfried is presented as not in control of his own fate. It is his *Rheinfahrt*, the Rhine Journey, his going out into the world and meeting civilisation, that corrupts him. Even upon his leaving the cave with Brünnhilde, he seems intent to leave her – an odd gesture for the basis of a love duet. I try to remind myself that Brünnhilde is his only real relationship. He always saw Mime as a nonentity compared to himself; Brünnhilde is the first and maybe only mature, reciprocal relationship – a person who has attributes other than merely being in his way. In the Prologue duet he echoes more than reciprocal love – more like the dissolving of self into the other: '*nicht Siegfried acht' ich mich mehr, ich bin nur Brünnhilde's Arm*'.[1]

So Siegfried has to realise his destiny. And Brünnhilde encourages him in that quest. That's why she puts all these runes on him, exercising her knowledge of *Zauberkraft*, magical power. With this knowledge that she gives to him comes the desire to go out and perform great deeds. She has given him the protection and knowledge to grow from a boy to a man. When he entered from the forest and questioned Mime, he was searching for his identity, his parentage. He receives his understanding of himself with Brünnhilde. Now he must go out and extend his heroic actions into the world. This is Lancelot or Quixote, destined to do great deeds.

One of the other problems I've had to confront is why he goes off alone. We know she can leave the *Fels* – Siegfried eventually brings her back to the Gibichung Hall. Why are they not sojourning in the world together? Indeed, one gets the sense that she expects him to return. Also, I've always played it that Siegfried is eager to go. But why? Is he bored? And why don't

[1] 'I am no longer Siegfried – I am Brünnhilde's arm.'

they have a child? And why does she give him Grane, who by now is merely a horse? And why does Siegfried want it? Why does Siegfried get off the boat to meet Gunther – what does he seek from the Gibichungs?

He is gone a long, long time. Between the duet and the opening of Act I proper is not a one-day journey. When he arrives, he says he seeks Gibich's son, which means he has heard from others of Gunther. So has Gunther heard of Siegfried, from Hagen? And when Siegfried asks Hagen how Hagen knew his name, Hagen replies I recognise you only by your power – I have heard of your mighty deeds. So legends have gotten around. During the time between his leaving the *Fels* and arriving onshore at Gibichung Hall, Siegfried has engaged with folks who explained to him the reputation of the Gibichung and, more problematically, Siegfried himself has performed public deeds that have become legend among the population of the Rhine. The only problem is that Wagner just didn't write any of this.

With the exception of the opening duet (one of the most glorious pieces of music Wagner wrote), little in the rest of the role is musically thrilling. It's an easier role to sing than the young Siegfried, but it's not gracious. The scene in Gibichung Hall is talky, and is really there only to set up the *Fels* scene at the end of the Act. The first serious decision a Siegfried has to make is in this scene, which is his interest in Gutrune. Is it the drink alone that makes him forget Brünnhilde, and does that automatically lead to his wanting to have sex with Gutrune? The minute Gutrune walks in, he is distracted by her and makes comments about her to her brother. I think the most likely choice is that Siegfried's character has already strayed from Brünnhilde before the drink.

Then there's the drink. Just before he drinks the potion, he steps aside to offer a private commemoration of Brünnhilde – that if he were to forget everything she gave him, the one thing he will never forget is his love for her. And of course he abruptly does.

To what degree is this supposed magic actually causing Siegfried's forgetting of Brünnhilde, or just giving him an excuse to bed Gutrune? Moments after the drink, the music does play the memory theme. But the actor must decide, is it the drink that prompts his unfaithfulness or the flaws in Siegfried's own character, developed during the time span between the departure from the *Fels* and his arrival at Gibichung? I choose the latter – it's the man's own flaws, not an external agent. The drink makes him forget the intent or purpose of Brünnhilde, but not who she is. You must play it like that, or Siegfried would come off as a complete cad. It would be impossible for him to have moral authority or heroic stature.

Perhaps you can say that the potion takes him back to the first time he saw a woman. He forgets that he saw a woman, but doesn't forget other things.

Stephen Gould as Siegfried in Götterdämmerung, *Bayreuth Festival, 2022*

Instant virginity. Fine slicing, and hard to enact on stage, but it does justify what follows. And even then, why does he not remember going through the fire before? These are questions to which not even the most persistent and imaginative questioning can provide answers that an actor can embody. So one must simply accept it: Siegfried has somehow been corrupted during the Rhine Journey and the days or months or years that followed. It took me many performances to come to this realisation. And it's compelled by Act II: you can't blame on the magic drink the fact that Siegfried tries to lie his way out of his predicament in the Second Act when confronted by Hagen, Gunther, Gutrune and Brunnhilde. He's worried about how he looks to the vassals. The drink makes him focus on Gutrune, more than it makes him forget Brünnhilde.

You have to ask yourself – the potion can change his memory but not his character. Here it's impossible not to concede that he agrees to deception: I will dissemble, force this woman on the *Fels*, into sexual slavery on your behalf, so that I can bed your sister. Deal? Deal.

Blutbrüderschaft – blood-brotherhood. This decision is not attributable to the potion. He has formed a nasty agreement with a spineless guy at the behest of his even nastier half-brother. Assuming it's a selective potion, where he retains other memories but not of Brünnhilde, this is nevertheless, inescapably, an agreement to deceive, to lie. And the nature of lies is that they get bigger and messier, which of course is what happens.

The first decision is in the potion scene; the second is at the end of the act when he takes her from the *Fels*. He says, I'm a hero and I've come to claim you and you will follow me now. He forcibly takes the ring off her, tantamount to rape, then at the end implies that he's going to use Nothung to separate them on the bridal night. But what does that mean? She says the power of this ring will keep you from me, and therefore he strips her of it. At the end of Act I, he calls on Nothung to bear witness that he has been honourable, that I have been faithful to my blood-brother, and separate me from his bride. And there is no reason not to take him at his word. But why does she not conclude that this must be Siegfried? Have the rules changed, and now someone else can brave the fire?

In Act II, in all candour, Siegfried's music is not that interesting to sing and he's a little schizophrenic to boot. He comes in and does a trio where he explains what has happened on the *Fels*. I've done what Gunther wanted, fulfilled my bargain, now let's go have sex. Gutrune is suspicious but he explains to her that Nothung kept them apart. And of course Hagen is interested in the details for a different reason: he sees the ring that Siegfried is now wearing, and that he wasn't wearing when he left.

Siegfried's returning to the *Fels* and taking the ring from Brünnhilde is bad enough; now we come to his denying the theft, but simultaneously keeping the ring. Since Siegfried went to the *Fels* in Gunther's stead, and took the ring on Gunther's behalf, why doesn't he give the ring to Gunther, when he gives him the woman? The ring, supposedly, is meaningless to Siegfried. He takes it only because she tells him that its power will prevent her rape. The same problem arises in Act III when he's playing with the nymphs: if the ring means nothing to him, why doesn't he just give it to them? He seems at one point to earnestly want to give them the ring, but they don't take it, saying that he should keep it: '*Behalt' ihn Held und wahr' ihn wohl...*'.[2] They seem to want to tell him about the curse on the ring but that doesn't matter to him; he already knows about the curse on the ring; Fafner told him so, as he himself relates to the nymphs.

Not long thereafter we have yet another problem. It starts off with the shock that Brünnhilde recognises him as Siegfried – besotted by the power of the potion, he (supposedly) thinks she has seen him only once, and only in the guise of Gunther. Then Brünnhilde says I see a ring on your hand; it doesn't belong to you, but rather to the man who took me from the *Fels*. Her subsequent reference to Nothung in Act II is shocking: I know that sword and I know the hilt it goes into. That is saying, I know your penile sword and my body was the hilt you put it into. In denial, Siegfried refers to last night's chastity and she refers to their lusty years in the cave; is this melodramatic miscommunication the stuff of heroic tragedy?

Siegfried is caught in a lie that brings out the worst in him. He could just easily give the ring to Gunther, but for some strange reason he doesn't. Until *Götterdämmerung* Siegfried was never one for deceit, but he is now caught in a web of lies that gets worse and worse during the scene. He says I got this ring from a dragon. Well, he knows that can't possibly be credible – he clearly knows that he took it from her just the night before. She says he's a liar: '*Du listiger Held, sieh' wie du lügst!*'[3] It's clear she's telling the truth. By now the performer of Siegfried is as mixed up as the character is: either his memory is coming back or he's starting to realise, yes, this ring did belong to me and I gave it to her and I took it back and.... But how do you play that? As an actor you confront impossible choices. At the end of Act I Siegfried takes the ring from Brünnhilde's finger. Then in Act II he tells people he got it from a dragon. A child trying to get out of brushing his teeth could do better than that. And note that he doesn't say he found it on the street; he says he got it *from a dragon*. That makes it even more difficult to perform – if he were a blatant liar, he would not have told the truth here;

[2] 'Keep it, hero, and guard it well.'
[3] 'You cunning hero, see how you lie!'

he would have made something up. It's as if Siegfried starts acting like Mime, speaking in half-truths rather than wholesale fabrications. Wagner needed a good *Dramaturg*.

It's this kind of problem that defies cogent performance. The problem lies in the character as written. At that point all I can do as a performer is play what is written, which is a two-faced guy, making frankly senseless and transparently self-defeating choices. Siegfried dismisses the entire conundrum and continues in his bravado, preparing for the wedding, insulting Brünnhilde as a wild *Felsenfrau*, a mountain woman. He never explains the ring; he never even tries. Whence Brünnhilde's ferocious anger, and that smashing trio.

I think sometimes that Wagner wrote such a flawed Siegfried character, simply so that the other three characters could have that trio. Each character is given the time needed for each to come to the individual conclusion that Siegfried must die. It is not only great music; it's great character-driven story-telling.

In the entire *Ring*, in all the roles written for the tenor like Mime and Froh and Siegmund and so on, there are a variety of ways to play the different characters. And even in *Götterdämmerung* the other characters are rich in their dramatic challenges and how they deal with the circumstances that surround them. But for Siegfried, the personality simply pales. When you encounter a role where there is really nothing to explore – or where exploration is stymied, leads to dead ends – then you fall back on the music. And fortunately it's pretty glorious. So at the end of Act II we have Siegfried having talked his way out of it, but he's actually entangled himself in the Norns' web inextricably. And Siegfried must die.

For me, the most challenging, but at the same time most enjoyable, part to sing is Act III. Here we see Siegfried after his wedding night, out on the celebratory hunt. He's joyous, carefree, and he immediately starts flirting with the Rhinemaidens in a pre-*Götterdämmerung* way – boyish, at liberty. His character is almost back to the beginning, with the bear – he finds things of nature and he enjoys engaging with them. The men come and he's very willing, with no coercion and very little prompting, to tell his story from the beginning. There is no complexity or depth of perception to this man – he is given the opportunity to review his life, and unwittingly thereby to provide Hagen with the provocation for murder that Hagen needs.

And note that, in this scene, with the potion still in full effect, Siegfried has no difficulty at all remembering the woodbirds he didn't understand, remembering Mime, the dragon, the ring, the Tarnhelm, the Woodbird he did understand. And it's at that moment he is given the antidote. It's almost like he's on the tip of remembering when he is given the second drink. And

Götterdämmerung, *Act III, Bayreuth Festival, 2022:
left to right, Simone Schröder (Flosshilde), Stephen Gould (Siegfried),
Lea-Ann Dunbar (Woglinde) and Stephanie Houtzeel (Wellgunde)*

now you have a gripping moment of genuine tragic inevitability. He drinks the second potion, the ravens take flight, and calamity is now inevitable. Siegfried remembers the emotion of seeing Brünnhilde's sleeping form, that she threw her arms around him, and he was held in her arms. He's reliving the ecstasy, not just the event. Wonderful scene-writing.

The final soliloquy is amazing. Little breaths coming out of him, yet still not a single indication of fear. So the question is raised: after all this, did Siegfried ever actually learn fear? I think not, ironically. He experienced confusion and uncertainty, but now, even at the very moment of his death, he experiences no fear. He's where he was at the end of *Siegfried* Act III: nothing's wrong. He returns to his natural state, which is no fear. None of Wotan's conniving, none of the dragon, not even the fear he thought he learned on the *Fels*. Indeed, he confesses even at the moment of his own extinction that he had not learned fear: '*und das Fürchten, ach! Das ich nie gelernt, das Fürchten, das du mich kaum gelehrt*'.[4] He dies not in fear or pain, but in the joy of remembering. Wake up, open your eyes. Greet me.

Even a role that is so bound by mythological constraints that it defies individual characterisation, like Lohengrin, compares favourably to the *Götterdämmerung* Siegfried. It is the least well-written of Wagner's

[4] 'And fear, alas, I never did learn fear from you.'

characters. There are times that you run into roles where you make a lot of narrative compromises and finally just sit back and say, I'm going to trust the composer and what's written here to make it come across. And of course it does.

As a performer, you make the best decisions you can, feeding a system of interpretation designed to work for you. And when you perform first the young Siegfried and the older one in the course of three days, you look back on the story you've told and conclude that it makes sense 'enough.' But had the details of Siegfried's narrative been worked out more clearly, it would be an easier role to perform.

There is a very satisfying circularity to the progress of the character. Siegfried starts out with no interest at all in the use of power to obtain objectives like wealth or control of others. In the course of the plays, he loses that indifference and agrees to engage in deceit to obtain certain ends. His regaining his sense of anarchic wonder, and ultimately ending in a state of ecstatic love, is entirely remarkable. It may be that the *Ring* teaches that corruption is inevitable. It may be that the next world, that succeeds the one depicted in the *Ring*, will start off pure but end in corruption. But Siegfried's story starts in innocence and ends in ecstasy.

IV
Lohengrin and Erik

I think of *Lohengrin* as an opportunity for Wagner to expand his orchestral skills and push ahead his remarkably creative, indeed epoch-making, musicianship. At the same time, to me, it displays perhaps disproportionately little advancement – even perhaps some regression – in his skill as a dramatist.

In *Lohengrin* it's clear to me that Wagner's still in his Italian, lyrical phase, not yet ready to create the distinctive sound that *Rheingold* reflects. The music in *Lohengrin* is sublime to sing and to listen to. And to his credit Wagner was always looking for mythology arising from Celtic and Teutonic traditions and history, though one might uncharitably conclude that this particular one was a clunker. And of course later, with *Parsifal,* we see that Wagner was finding a lot of his material with this use of myth (or, in the case of *The Flying Dutchman*, broadly recognised folk-tales), while not sacrificing dramatic nuance and expansive opportunities for characterisation.

In this score, too, he is still investigating tone-painting – still trying to find a sonic balance between the sung narrative and the orchestra. Musically, *Lohengrin* is in many ways quite revolutionary. Indeed, performing *Lohengrin* for me has always been about the music. I am never challenged by the story because really there is no story, in the sense of something happening to the protagonist as a result of the circumstances that occur during a plot involving conflict. While it is a very strange piece, with very strange personalities, Lohengrin as a dramatic role is almost a nonentity.

In the course of preparing it, I thought, wow, this guy is really pathetic. 'I'm here to save, in service of truth and justice, this woman who, at least possibly, is insane or psychotic, and who perhaps has killed her brother.' Think of it: she might be a murderer. We know nothing. It is entirely ambiguous. And Lohengrin seems to have no social or dramatic function or utility independent of his job of redeeming her. There's no indication that he was busy the day before or the day after he decided (or was sent) to save her.

And the incredible nature of this entire enterprise only gets worse. What is this garbage about you can't know my name? Has any performer ever made dramatic sense of that? (By which I mean, can anybody fit that utterance into a sensible, causal narrative of events?) And he later tells us – in this *fantastic* aria – that, oh, he can only do these wonderful acts if someone loves him so much that they agree to remain completely ignorant or else he will have to flee back to wherever, and by the way with respect to the whole reason the curtain went up, which was for Henry the Fowler to raise an army against invading hordes from the East, he couldn't possibly be bothered other than to return to them a child who used to be a swan. I mean, it's just as bad as a typical Verdi plot. Worse even. At least no one throws the wrong baby into the bonfire,[1] but still....

Nevertheless, the story is of a piece with – indeed an advancement on – Wagner's continuing theme of a man's experiencing salvation through the agency of a woman. Mind you, if you think about it, here it's the woman who seeks to be rescued through the agency of a redemptive man. Wagner's personal psychosis is evident here, which is of interest in itself. So, you put all these things together and you have one of Wagner's most uninteresting plots, one of the most pathetic, really. There's nobody who is noble. There's nobody whose motives are without suspicion. And even Ortrud's character seems out of a cartoon – she's just over-the-top Evil. Just as Lohengrin is a Dudley Do-Right[2] who is either morally so unimaginative as to be irrelevant, or else just plain obtuse. I understand when some people say that it's not one of their favourite pieces. But musically – particularly from the perspective of the tenor, the lead role, and the powerful Ortrud – it is simply, without interruption, glorious.

Hidden dangers lurk: Telramund, it may come as a surprise to many to learn, is a very difficult role that many baritones have ruined their voices trying to sing. It's one of the Wagner roles that can lead to the conclusion that some Wagner can't be sung. That is not true, but you have to be careful, and many baritones are not. It is a very percussive role. In some ways it is like the young Siegfried – there are sporadic opportunities to produce *legato* lines, but for the most part it is hard-hitting, percussive language. You start to see, in *Lohengrin*, Wagner wanting the language to be as important as the music and intentionally selecting utterances for their musical impact. And this aesthetic is first introduced, in this transitional period, in the evil characters.

In recent years people have tried to deconstruct *Lohengrin*, trying to experiment with making the evil characters less evil and the virtuous characters more complicated. And that's legitimate. Here you have a piece where Wagner has given you relatively nothing, and I think it's open season to try to find out what might be there. Even *Dutchman*, even *Rienzi*, has a more interesting story and more nuanced characterisations.

But keep in mind that this is a stage in the artist's progression. Wagner didn't come out of a vacuum – he always expected his music, even if it was

---

[1] A reference to the plot of Verdi's *Il trovatore*.
[2] Another US cartoon character, the well-meaning but obtuse 'Dudley Do-Right of the Mounties' was first seen in a segment of *The Rocky and Bullwinkle Show* in 1959.

IV: Lohengrin and Erik

more 'talky', to be sung in the Italian style. *Bel canto* was still the expected sound on the stage. The voices were going to have to be modified a little bit, true; but *Lohengrin* and *Dutchman* show his compositional skills moving away from the traditional – even though, as I suggest, the drama is perhaps not as progressive as the music. And we see him still trying to find the right stories to embrace this new chromaticism he's exploring.

Not until the *Ring* do all of these elements find a felicitous unity. And in a way, that integration of creative thought did not even start with the first note of the *Ring*. Not until *Tristan* did Wagner really finish his compositional development. In *Tristan* Wagner said here is my musical power. Here are my brushes and my paint, here is all that I need to create my perfect art – I have perfected it in *Tristan*. Now I can sit here and play. And he did the glorious *Meistersinger*, got the rest of the *Ring* behind him, and then wrote *Parsifal*.

One aspect of this continuing musical development that *Lohengrin* exemplifies is uniquely evident when you perform it. There is absolutely a difference between standing on the stage and singing Tannhäuser with its orchestration and singing Lohengrin with its orchestration. In *Tannhäuser* (and especially in *Tristan*) one gets the occasional feeling onstage that there are these walls, these intense waves of sound that are so thick that Wagner intends for you to mix with that, to become one instrument among many, and to abandon the job of being on top of it, accompanied and supported by it as is more generally the case when you're acting a part in a story. And that requires the tenor to accept that you should avoid the temptation of doing what other operas expect you to do, and try to over-sing the orchestra. This was an entirely new approach to performing opera, and remains a distinctive one to this day.

In *Lohengrin*, by contrast, that's not the case. That 'wall of sound' never appears. The role of Lohengrin is written so that all that music can surge below and you can ride right on top of it. It's still very *bel canto*. In that sense, it is ironically a challenge sometimes for a bigger voice – and that's why currently the proponents of the role tend to have lighter and lighter voices: because they can, and because it fits.

After the posturing and heroics of Act I, Act II is the scene before the church, not a lot of meat to chew on there. Act III is everything for Lohengrin. You can argue that the dramatic action of Act III mirrors Wagner, in his own personal life, fighting the demons of his own feelings of inadequacy, wanting to love a strong woman but not being able to find satisfaction in that expectation, slaying his enemies but still not attaining his goal. Indeed, looking at the progress – or lack thereof – of the character, we have Lohengrin who, in order to have a personal relationship, has to create this artificial and really inhuman set of rules and regulations that he and Elsa must follow. And of course she fails, and of course so does he. She fears this figure. Does she fear that he is going to find out that she is a murderer? Or is she just simple? This is why the plot is so difficult for some people.

Erik in *Der fliegende Holländer* is a difficult role for different reasons. First, because it's so short. And second, Erik can easily appear as the Don Ottavio of the Wagner world: a very weak, almost pathetic man, whose happiness is entirely dependent on Senta, and spending his stage time following her around. If you're not careful, Erik can come off as a whining *nudnik*. He's never welcome. He's not reflective or analytical. It's not important, when performing the dramatic action that Erik is charged with, for him to possess a sophisticated understanding of his relationship either to the Dutchman or to Senta. But ironically, I eventually discovered that the success of the role derives from just these seeming limitations – assuming and exhibiting independence, strength and power.

When I first did the part, I did it because I could. Many singers have the chops to do the *cabaletta*[3] but not all have the power at the end. I can give the Third Act trio the right power. But I never thought I'd sing it that much – I mean, who wants to pay the fee of a Heldentenor to sing the role of Erik? But some do. So I've sung it about 70 times, and I still sing it – in Bayreuth 2021 I was covering it and did the dress rehearsal, though I hadn't sung it in three or four years, and I was pleased to realise that it was still all there.

Erik is really a dramatic part. It's just that *cabaletta* that distracts people sometimes in terms of the type of role. He's in over his head in some ways – everyone onstage has more going for him or her than Erik does. Indeed, the part works best if you're somewhat simple, if you know nothing about the Dutchman and if you misunderstand Senta entirely.

It fell into place with me recently, when I ran into a production, in Munich, by Peter Konwitschny.[4] It was staged in a very brutal way where Senta is no wallflower – she's a psychotic, abused woman herself. When you think about it, the driving condition under which the characters centrally make choices is that Senta's father is trying to sell her. So Konwitschny's idea was that there had to be a strong love/hate triangle for the piece to work.

---

[3] A two-part aria in which the first part has a definite rhythmic emphasis and the second part is quick and often virtuosic.
[4] This production had its premiere at the Bayerische Staatsoper in 2012, conducted by Kazushi Ono. Alan Held took the role of the Dutchman, Klaus Florian Vogt that of Erik, and Anja Kampe that of Senta.

IV: Lohengrin and Erik

The Dutchman is not in love with Senta; indeed, he has never even laid eyes on her, but rather wants to buy her in order to use her as an agency to expiate the curse under which he labours. And in return Senta is (or can be) someone who fights, who will not be controlled by her father or even by the Dutchman, and certainly not by Erik. She is not romantically enraptured by the Dutchman as a person, but rather by his myth. His mythology affords her the ultimate opportunity to go against her father and even, perhaps, kill herself as a final gesture of disassociation. And finally, here is Erik: a hunter, a strong-willed man from his village, the ultimate Eligible Bachelor with Options. Senta has put him off and now her father has found a much wealthier man to sell her off to. So he's angry. He's aggressive. He's a typical toxic male with entitlement: Senta belongs to me and if she won't come to me by agreement, I'll force her. They're all strong-willed, damaged characters. You put that dynamic together, and it really starts to work. All the characters take over like kudzu.[5]

And the music – just because there's longing in some of it – becomes aggressive, too. Invested with muscle, the *cabaletta* becomes aggressive – how can you do this to me? And when Erik and the Dutchman finally see each other, invective erupts and flows. The Dutchman asks, you've given me up for this nothing? And Erik says how can you do this to me, going with a man who is pure evil? And Senta is saying the two of you are idiots. Which in many ways they are, at least as far as she's concerned. Raising the stakes gives sinew to the play.

The music is great. The entrance of the Dutchman in Act I is one of the most glorious through-composed monologues that Wagner has made, and all the more impressive because he made it very early on in his career.

When we hold *Lohengrin* against *Dutchman*, we see two examples of Wagner investigating the balance of the poetry and words, on the one hand, against the mighty imagination of the musical content. He was always searching. Still, you simply can't ignore the dramatic incompetence of that later work. When making the first entrance, Lohengrin is saying I'm going to take this swan from the *ferne Land*, the 'distant land', to Antwerp, and what I'm going to do there is to lock horns with this baritone in order to have this soprano vindicated and, if things work out, well, I'll stay and marry her and have kids and if they don't work out, well, I'll get back on the swan and go home. That's perhaps unfair but it's not an overstatement, and it's certainly not inaccurate as you're standing in the wings ready to enter. And it's hard to play that set of circumstances if you hope to portray anything like a recognisable human being. Despite all I've read and the traditions of

---

[5] A vine in the genus Pueraria (and pea family Fabaceae), sometimes called Chinese or Japanese arrowroot, that has become an invasive species in North America.

performance, he's the most mono-dimensional of Wagner's tenor heroes. I can't decide whether he's supernatural – obviously he is in terms of how he got his power – or a super-hero or an anti-hero or a Daddy's boy or a guy with a redemption complex or what. It's hard playing him without being almost a stick figure. Oddly, the last time I played Lohengrin it was, again, a Konwitschny production staged in Hamburg in 1998. I'd heard about it before I joined it – he staged it in a school, where all the community were students, kids, and Lohengrin was the teacher. He's the only adult in the group. And despite my initial misgivings, it worked. Because it allowed the fairy-tale element to be played through the children and it gave Lohengrin the *gravitas* among the community that he needed in order to take the dramatic choices that Wagner requires be taken.

There is no solution. It's an interesting but stilted drama. I feel that you just have to look at it more on a mythological scale, or a morality play, as opposed to a cogent narrative. As I say, I was never challenged on an intellectual or emotional or ethical level the way I am in everything else I've encountered in Wagner. But the singing of the part is pretty noble. And that ultimately took over. I'm here as a supernatural hero, I'm here to correct the wrongs and bring balance back to this society and to the interpersonal dealings the other characters had thrown amiss. He's the only person on the stage whose intentions are pure. He's something of a manic depressive, true. He says in the beginning he's an agent of truth and justice and at the end leaves in utter despair. If you took a more human perspective, you'd ask yourself whether there's something missing in him, that he's someone who needs to be a saviour, or that he's looking at other people as opportunities to get something out of them.

But really, the role is not helped by pursuing that avenue – with him or with any of them. For example, do we really want to examine the logic of Elsa's spending the rest of her life huddled up with somebody that she not only doesn't know, but has agreed never to know, as an exercise in 'trust'? And what is he saying to Heinrich: I won't help you, I won't lead your army, I won't save your country from the invaders, I've saved Elsa but she blew it and I'm out of here, but here's a kid in my place? It's pathetic. The last sung word in the play is '*Wehe*', and the last action is that Elsa – who was meant to be the object of vindication – dies. Perhaps if I'd played this role as often as I sang Tristan or Siegfried I might have tried harder to work this out. But I must tell you I just don't see it. In my career, Lohengrin has always been about pure singing pleasure. And as I say, it's a wow.

Some things don't reward analysis. Once you're in the realm of super-heroes, and you embrace it and just go ahead and perform the role, you don't ask whether Robin has a zipper on the back of his pants so he can

IV: Lohengrin and Erik

Stephen Gould as Lohengrin, Semper Oper, Dresden, 2006

poop. When you're dealing with Erik or Siegmund, there's a character there, in a situation, with needs and challenges and different ways to go about it. With Lohengrin you have to just embrace the frozen statue for what it is: something for other people to look at and react to. They represent something rather than being someone in their own right.

You are best off just going out there and singing it. Then everybody's happy, including you.

V
Parsifal

I first tackled Parsifal early. It was always planned to be my first Wagner role, so I did concert excerpts from *Parsifal* a lot from the beginning, I think 1999. Parsifal and Siegmund are the introductory roles because they're very low. The highest note in both is a high A and it comes only once.

Also for Parsifal they want a young man, which, I have come to think, may be false. Just because he's the *reine Tor* ('pure fool') doesn't mean he's necessarily a teenager. His mother has kept him isolated for a long time and kept him away from weapons and things like this because she doesn't want him to end up with the same fate as his father. He's naïve, yes, and he's virginal, but I have always seen him as being on the verge of middle age, from late twenties to late thirties. Because then it's interesting. In Act I it's interesting that Gurnemanz doesn't recognise that he is a *reiner Tor*. They are thinking of a young novitiate, and they don't recognise him if, as I suggest, he's an adult. They also fail to realise that the *reine Tor* is going to be their leader.

Parsifal is not stupid. We think of a *Tor* as being a fool, but I believe Wagner's sense is that he is a fool in the sense of Shakespeare's fool: he is the person with a natural sense of wisdom, and perhaps he himself doesn't know it. The Shakespeare fools act as clowns, to amuse; but they are the ones who show us the real inner meaning of the characters and the events and choices made in the play. And I think this is the nature of Parsifal.

So, although he doesn't have to be super-young, and indeed his being older feeds some important aspects of the drama, nevertheless they usually cast the role with younger voices, more lyrical voices, because they want this youth.

When I first learned it and started to perform it, it felt good to me. My teacher, John Fiorito,[1] used certain sections as teaching tools. The great *arioso* in Act II, '*Amfortas, die Wunde*', was my introduction to the declamatory nature of Wagner text. *Parsifal* was Wagner's last piece, so musically – from the tone and the colours – this is the epitome of Wagner's mature style. The score seems to float among tonalities and snippets of melodies with a confidence and sophistication surpassing even *Tristan*, and it might leave a young, inexperienced singer – without the benefit of knowing the earlier

---

[1] Born in New York in 1936, John Fiorito first sang with the New York City Opera in 1961, before becoming a leading baritone with the (touring) Metropolitan Opera National Company, retiring after fifteen seasons to concentrate on teaching.

roles – feeling a bit Schoenberg-like, a little foreign and challenging when trying to learn it.

Before the Second World War you would never have a young singer do Parsifal. When you looked at the *Fach*[2] book, this was a Heldentenor piece. Tristan and Parsifal are listed as requiring the same vocal colour. Most likely the proponents of the role in those days came from the darker colours. What changed was the availability of the proper voice to sing it, and the introduction of the approach of Wieland Wagner,[3] this deconstruction of the works.

Look at Melchior. He sang so many performances of everything – *Ring*, *Tristan*, *Tannhäuser* – at the Met and elsewhere. But wherever he sang, the staging was always the same as the staging used in Bayreuth. No matter where the house, they had the same set, the same costumes, props. When you came to the Met to sing the *Ring*, you would have two or three days to rehearse because they assumed you knew the Bayreuth staging. Theatre really did change after the Second World War.

So out of this earlier period came the tradition of having certain voices – darker, more experienced voices – come to Parsifal and Tristan and Tannhäuser. I think that may be why some people find Tannhäuser so difficult to sing, because they wait until after they've done all these other things before they do Tannhäuser. Then they say it's one of the most difficult roles to sing. Well, it is if the wrong kinds of tenors try to sing it, and do so too late in their careers. I had the good fortune to have a teacher who said, no, Tannhäuser has a lot of lyricism in it. You need to sing Tannhäuser before you sing Tristan, before you sing these things.

Even Parsifal. I had trouble with Act III of Parsifal, the first time I did it, because it's low, and it's very declamatory. And I had not yet learned this *gesamt* style which Wagner invented and introduced in the *Ring*. It's a whole new way of singing – like singing recitatives with a full orchestra under you rather than a harpsichord. For me, I was preparing to do my first Parsifal because I came from a lower baritonal sound, and this would be an easier introduction for me into Wagner.

It had some challenges to it, but I was very fortunate. I did my first full production of *Parsifal* in 2003, in Graz, with Philippe Jordan. We were all doing our roles for the first time and we had a grand time. It was a

---

[2] In German opera houses, 'Fach' is a traditional way of classifying singers by type of voice and corresponding role.

[3] The grandson of Richard (and thus great-grandson of Franz Liszt), Wieland Wagner (1917–66) was co-director (with his brother Wolfgang) of the Bayreuth Festival from its post-War re-opening in 1951 until his early death. He was one of the progenitors of *Regietheater*, rejecting the naturalist settings of earlier productions in favour of more radical and symbolic approaches.

modern, weird production that illuminated the story. And we got a lot of repetition – we did maybe ten or twelve performances. When you do a run that long, you can really start to get a role into your body and your mind. Then I did it in Dresden and other places, like Baden-Baden with Simon Rattle. So I've probably done Parsifal between 30 and 40 times.

The last time I performed it, in concert in Bayreuth in 2021, it seemed most simple and straightforward. This simplicity is not evident when you first engage with the role. What happens to the character might seem challenging for an audience member to follow. When we meet him, he seems not even to know his own name, and cannot find words to express his emotions. He is sexually teased and seduced but refuses carnal engagement. Then he assumes almost demi-god proportions, having gained wisdom, perspective and a capacity to forgive and to heal, taking on the responsibility of king and priest. It's in many ways the most difficult Wagner tenor role for some audiences to follow.

The 2021 concert performance was an extraordinary occasion; Covid had derailed the organisation. The 2020 Festival had been cancelled, the 2021 Festival had only half the tickets available, and this was the year we were trying to save the Festival. Every person on the stage had lived with their roles and knew what their job was, how they fitted, not only in the play but in the Festival itself. For me personally, for the first time I was able to sing the role with no sense of naïveté or spiritual gift or nobility or trying to put on some kind of mythological presence. I suddenly realised that when, through agencies of fate and faith, Parsifal takes over leadership of the *Gesellschaft*, it is not a moment of triumph, but rather an inevitable transformation and acceptance of suffering. I felt the weight of current events, what was happening around me with this beautiful Festival, and my friends, and myself, the pressure of the times in which we were living, and I reflected on my career, realising that I am a singer who spends perhaps a bit more time delving into my assigned role, feeling the character rather than simply performing the character. This had led to some criticism to my way of singing, but there are a lot of people who are moved by that. It goes back to my conviction that if I am on the stage and I am not discovering something about the character right then – while I am performing – then I shouldn't expect anyone in the audience to be moved, or to discover something themselves.

So that evening, that afternoon, I was indeed charged. It happened at a certain moment of need, and of release. Petra Lang's Kundry was not just sung, but personified, displayed. She knows that character through and through. *Parsifal* is not a calm piece; it is a transcendent piece. It has so much Buddhism and Schopenhauer that it's hard to ignore the profound pulse at the core of it. The audience often doesn't really sense that, but it's hard for the performers to avoid. We were in concert, and as I tried to tell the story through the text I also felt the weight of Parsifal himself saying, I'm taking over this duty from you. You are released from it, and from this hellish life you have been living. '*Sei heil entsündigt und entsühnt!*'[4] And when you think of that, the mystical grail is not there to heal us – when he says that, we are going back now. 'I am assuming your suffering. And through suffering we will eventually transcend.' It's almost, as I like to think, taking Christian philosophy and melding it with Buddhist philosophy. Because it all leads to the same place.

Perhaps it's easier to understand the story than to understand the character. The reason Parsifal is a *reiner Tor* from the beginning is beyond naïve. It enters into the realm of the impossible. Here is a man who has been raised by a mother in fear of life itself, who has been separated and almost been isolated, physically, emotionally, spiritually. He's of noble birth, meant to be a knight, but his mother has tried to prevent that. He basically runs away from home at some point – not because he is rebelling from parental control, or out of any developed philosophy or ambition, quite the contrary. He runs because he's a naïve fool, distracted by a bright and shiny object. He sees dandies ride by on horses, and he runs out after them. He keeps running until he loses himself.

And that's our allegory. He's a lost soul, lost in himself because of himself. Further, he loses himself 'in' the world, because he has no experience being 'of' the world. Parsifal has to lose much of himself to even accidentally discover this mystical land of Monsalvat. He has to lose a certain part of himself to develop even to the state of a *Tor*, even to get in the door. He lacks even the most primitive moral instinct or instruction. Compare: Siegfried would never kill a swan for the fun of it. But it needs to be pointed out to Parsifal that such an act is morally reprehensible. Parsifal immediately learns the rudimentary difference between right and wrong, in front of us.

Parsifal shoots swans because he's good at it – to shoot fowl in the air with an arrow, not an easy task. He was not allowed to fight; he was not allowed to learn the life of a knight because it's a life that his father led and that his mother is keeping him from. So what he learns, he learns by going in one certain direction until he bumps, then altering course until he bumps into the next thing. He has to develop. I like to look at his journey as errant, not intended. That's why he forgets his name. He didn't run away; he just got lost.

---

[4] 'Be whole, healed and forgiven!'

V: Parsifal

So when he is taken to Monsalvat, he's exposed to something that should provoke empathy in a developed sensibility, but not in Parsifal. He just gapes at it. He doesn't understand this bleeding from the thigh, the highly ritualistic exposure of the Grail, the symbolism, the communal meal, the societal context, the wounded king. Being human ordinarily involves social ritual, but those lessons have been denied Parsifal. Parsifal has no context for this peculiar group-behaviour going on in front of him, because he has been intentionally denied it. He is the *reine Tor,* yes, but he is still nowhere near ready to take up the ultimate suffering that will lead to the ultimate transcendence. He must journey from his mother to the forest; from the forest to Monsalvat; from Monsalvat to Klingsor's *Zaubergarten*, his Magic Garden; from Klingsor through the wilderness back to the forest; and finally from the forest back to Monsalvat.

And this journey, this process of accumulation of knowledge through compassionate suffering, was the prophecy: not merely that the *reine Tor* would redeem us, but that he would do so '*durch Mitleid, wissend*'.[5] The community is looking for salvation through the promised *reine Tor* and it is not surprising that Gurnemanz invites him to the castle. But Parsifal is incapable of expressing his emotions in response to what he witnesses, and this frustrates Gurnemanz: if you're not the agent of our salvation, then get out. What does Parsifal see? Visions. Inchoate images. He sees visions of the suffering of Christ, the suffering of the people, past efforts of redemption, the glow, the pulse, the blood.

And these visions echo against themselves. In Act II, he is told that Kundry laughed, not at Christ, but at the possibility of redemption. She lacked the seed of her own salvation: the willingness to experience the suffering of others. *Mitleid.* The unpardonable sin in Christian theology is blaspheming the Holy Spirit. Blasphemy is not a discrete act; it's a state of mind: the denial of the power of God. You can't be forgiven for constantly denying God himself, denying the possibility of redemption.

Why did Parsifal go to a distant land, upon being ejected from Monsalvat, and appear on a rampart and do battle with soldiers, killing and wounding them, before entering Klingsor's *Zaubergarten*? The waves of time and of destiny force Parsifal, unknowingly, in the same direction that Amfortas took, giving Parsifal the opportunity to succumb to, or to avoid, the same mistake of the flesh. He goes with the current, the world river that takes him away from the island and he happens to meet up with the great evil mythological magician.

---

[5] 'Coming to knowledge through compassion'.

Klingsor is in some ways Amfortas' twin, like Wotan and Alberich. It's all part of the Buddhist emphasis on opposites. And Kundry seduces Parsifal though that great magical power, guilt. She summons his mother and holds out to him the opportunity of forgiveness for the harm he did to her by his abandonment. She frames an erotic kiss as a maternal gift, and it is no wonder that he accepts it.

Then comes the great pivot. He doesn't just remember Amfortas – he *feels* Amfortas. He sees the vision of the temptation away from the heart, the blood flowing, the sacrifice that is made, the mockery of that sacrifice, the total suffering and pain that it means to be human. Later he says to Kundry, I've seen this look, I've heard this voice calling. And it has not called only me; every single human being has been ensnared in this nonreality that is the present. This is the great transformative moment. It's taken me years to realise it: it is at this moment, where Parsifal does not succumb but instead is transformed by the great universal vision, this is the moment that he becomes, not just a *Tor*, but a *reiner Tor*. It's not just Kundry; the other flower maidens have tried to seduce him, to take his chastity. So it is not sexual chastity that Parsifal reaffirms – it is the vision of pain, sacrifice, others' suffering, and taking on his responsibility for other people. The vision is the pain and suffering – *die Wunde* – not merely of Amfortas, but of all humanity.

And, finally, he fully sees Kundry not as a temptress, but as the tool by which this happens. She starts to argue back and forth but from that moment on, Parsifal knows what he has to do. She pleads with him: if you want to relieve someone of suffering, relieve me of mine. A good argument on its face. But Parsifal instructs her that she has to follow the path back to Amfortas. You have to redeem yourself. You have to continue your suffering. Parsifal thinks he will go back to the community – he doesn't perceive that it is a long path from enlightenment to the end of suffering. She is now on her journey back, as is he.

Curiously, Kundry has no trouble finding her way back to Monsalvat. He, by contrast, spends (I think) decades trying to get there. When he arrives, the community's suffering is at its greatest. It is spiritually exhausted. Death and isolation have taken over the kingdom. He does not rejoice when he arrives; he looks for engagement, service and healing.

There is an odd sense of dénouement throughout Act III. The climactic event has already occurred, and we are now witnessing its necessary consequence. One gets the sense of simply sliding effortlessly and inevitably to the end. It's quite remarkable dramaturgically – usually one brings things to a head during the last act towards a climax. Here, once Parsifal enters early in the act, it is all an unhindered flow towards redemption. He has

V: Parsifal

never allowed the spear to be defiled by violence; he delivers it whole and unsullied, as an agency of the release of suffering. He has come through the crucible, a finely tuned, spiritually balanced and tempered soul.

He expresses two events of regret: one because, had he arrived sooner, he might have forestalled Titurel's death; and the other, that he had arrived on *Karfreitag*, Good Friday, the most sorrowful day. Gurnemanz responds in a prudent and curative way, providing a realignment. He teaches that nature itself reaffirms the virtue of suffering, and the blessings that it yields.

Gurnemanz himself has become wiser. It would be easy for him to beat himself up for not recognizing the *reine Tor* but now he realises it's been his fated journey. You can't transcend this life until you have walked down the path. He's not so much correcting Parsifal as realising himself that, however much grief flows from Titurel's death, that too was Titurel's path.

And *Karfreitag*, Good Friday, is affirmation of renewal, before their eyes. The world blooms again, inevitably. The suffering of the world is not your fault; it had to happen in order for life to reassert itself. Once Parsifal realises this, having suffered, he is presented with the occasion to submit to the propriety of anointment: Kundry's ritualistic anointing his feet, and Gurnemanz's anointing him as king.

And he sees that, as the world awakens, Kundry's tears will convert to laughter, and Amfortas' despair will convert to service. Suffering yields to renewal. And I will be king. It's not that I have been vested with all power, but rather that I have returned nature and humanity to its natural state. Through this state, all people will transcend suffering.

Parsifal thereupon gives meaning to the lives of the community through the reinstatement of ritual. That ritual, in its absence, almost destroyed Monsalvat. Upon its reinstatement, it revives it.

Now let's drill down into the layer that really matters when playing this role. '*Durch Mitleid wissend, der reine Tor*'. *Mitleid* means, not to pity others for their suffering, but to 'feel with' them. Parsifal is gifted with (or earns) the ability to join others' suffering. He feels it, he internalises it. It is a state of complete, total understanding of a suffering that seems to be un-transcendable, but that he transcends. Remember, too, that it is '*durch*' – 'through', 'by means of'. It is a process, a state of being that is dynamic and that yields the state of '*wissend*', knowing. The remarkable power of *Mitleid* is that it is an agency leading to an end, not an end of its own.

This is why rejecting Kundry is so essential. I've been in productions where the *regisseur* wanted Parsifal to succumb to Kundry, actually fuck her. And I remember saying no, I can't do that. It's not about changing the character or shedding light on something else; there is no opera, we

Parsifal, *Act III*, Semper Oper, Dresden, 2005:
left to right, Evelyn Herlitzius (Kundry), Stephen Gould (Parsifal) and Kurt Rydl (Amfortas)

can't do anything else, if that happens. No. There has to be a redemptive act somewhere or there is no story. And that act has to have something to do with 'with/feel'. Some moment after which Parsifal feels all suffering. Many people experience pity, or can see others' suffering, but we're not talking about that. We're talking about entering someone else's suffering so completely that it becomes your own. That really is the story of Christ as God-Made-Flesh, or why in Buddhism you have avatars who come down to feel what it is to be human. It is so metaphysical as to be nearly incomprehensible. That moment – rejecting the carnal and erupting with 'Amfortas' – is so intense because, for that moment, he *is* Amfortas. He literally becomes Amfortas. And Parsifal (like Christ) takes on himself the sacrificial duty to expunge and then to lead. He has found his own inner redemption and becomes the agency of healing of others. It helps me as a performer, at least, that in *Lohengrin* he says his father, Parsifal, has sent him to cure. It feeds me.

The Grail grants sustenance, power and acceptance. Though he instructs that he is to be anointed '*König*', Parsifal is not the king of power or armies or of anything, at the end. He is the person who returned the spear, brought wholeness to the community, and enabled life to return to the *Gesellschaft*.

That's how I look at it. And as somebody who performs the role – and as somebody who is getting old himself, and tired – that's how I would play it. Parsifal does not – and we cannot – reach our salvation through intellect, or lust, or power. Indeed, we cannot control even our own destinies in the most essential ways. What we can do is look for the Grail. And the Grail will bring suffering but, *through* it, transcendence.

Like Tristan, Parsifal is a spiritually exhausting character. It's the shortest tenor role in all of Wagner, but the one that requires the greatest amount from the performer in terms of character development and narrative discipline. Parsifal's core condition is only scarcely real – he is a spiritual psyche trapped in a life that makes no sense, and that only transcendence can answer. If there is a lesson in it, it is that only to the extent that we care about each other that we can find meaning.

It's the height of irony that this came from a man who was focused and obsessed by only himself and his art. But that doesn't trouble me. You take the truth where you find it. There doesn't have to be coherence between an artist's behaviour and the art he creates.

VI
Working with Conductors and Stage Directors

Tenors in the first five or ten years of a promising career may come across a conductor or a stage director whom they perceive as 'difficult'. And indeed, they may be correct – there are, out there, some conductors and directors, or designers, many of them hugely talented and gifted, who are indeed difficult to collaborate with. But it is in how one chooses to handle these challenges that the opportunity to learn, to grow and (of course) to advance professionally is to be found.

Months before I was to enter rehearsals for the Bayreuth 2019 *Tannhäuser*, I was scheduled for a wig-fitting. When I arrived, I was fitted for a clown wig. This was all I knew of the production concept at this point. What did I do? I put on the wig and waited for the Concept meeting. And that turned out to be (at least in my experience) a spectacularly insightful, innovative and successful production.

But I behave now differently from when I was a novice. When I entered my career, I knew I would run into a lot of *Regietheater*. I knew what my worth was, though. I was there to contribute, and I was also there to be engaged as an equal participant in the process. And for young singers coming in, often they go to extremes: either we're so insecure that we do anything they say without question, or else we're so assertive that we push back and say this is ridiculous and I won't do it or even try.

Both ways are wrong. There's a way to be strong and self-assertive, and yet be fair and open to new things. There's always conflict between the *regisseur* and the performers. The question before you is whether that conflict is – or can be transformed into – a creative one. If you find yourself working with a 'difficult' stage director, the thing to do is to engage with that artist. Put it on the table. You say, look, I don't understand this. I don't understand what you're asking me to do. And if they do explain it and you disagree with the concept, then the two of you have to come to some mediated understanding of how far you are willing to go. Sometimes – and very rarely, I emphasise – you may be asked to do things that you just cannot do. Putting on a clown wig, frankly, is not one of them. I'm talking about standing naked or doing something vulgar and reprehensible to your being. That happens so seldom that it's not really worth talking much about.

Keep in mind, too, that you are there under contract, and contracts are written to the advantage of the *regisseur*, not the performer. You have agreed to represent the vision of the director in the course of advancing the season of the producing organisation. If you go too much against it, that's contrary to the terms you agreed to and it's grounds for them to let you go. If you're already an established performer, it's harder for them to let you go, but we've all read of famous singers who have 'left productions' for 'artistic reasons'. We all know what happened: they had a big fight with the director or conductor and they lost. The house is usually going to come down on the side of the stage director and musical director. And you are a member of the performing company, and actor/singer that the organisation has engaged, not a stage director.

Directing an opera is entirely different from directing for the legitimate stage or for TV or film. Some opera directors understand that difference, and others do not. Sometimes there are stage directors who come into the rehearsal room at an opera house with only a general idea of what they want and have not yet worked out specifics. People who come from the straight theatre or – worse – cinema can be problematic in this sense. They have worked out a little beforehand, they have a sense what the work means, but they're used to sitting around a circle and reading the thing through several times and figuring out what undiscovered nuances may be in the text, or what the individual performer has to offer that was unexpected. And during this process, where the actors are trying things out, and perhaps the playwright is there revising for clarity, they all come to a sense of what they want to do. And that's great with a theatre piece – you have time to do that and work things through. And you can change some things that you did on Monday and try new ideas again on Wednesday.

In opera, that's not practical for a variety of reasons. One, the composer has given you (for the most part) what he or she expects, in the music. We can all give our flavours, colours to an interpretation musically, but that fundamental attribute is pretty much written with a specificity that a dramatic script doesn't possess. The music itself also has its own performance time. In straight theatre you can modify the way you say a sentence, how fast or slow, how loudly or softly, whether in cynicism or anger, whether you come in dead on-cue or pause to reflect or to do stage business. This is left up to the individual to decide in collaboration with others. In opera, by giving you the theatre-time the composer has taken many options away from the interpreter. The sentence that you say in response to another character's line or action is sung at a given pitch, and a given tempo, and a given rhythm, and a given dynamic. You may have a coloration here, a coloratura there, that indicates something but excludes many other things; in performance you have to find something that the coloratura indicates about the character or the situation or the emotional event. But all of these decisions must comply with, and be expressed within, the actual theatre time that is set by the composer's score.

VI: Working with Conductors and Stage Directors

What that means is that, when it comes to the person charged with setting the whole thing up, and deciding how things are going to work onstage in collaboration with everything else, that person must come in knowing what the vision is and how they are going to achieve it. Of course, things will change, that's how theatre works. But you have to have a master plan. You can't come to opera and use rehearsal to investigate internal motivations for each character, feeling for decisions that we can discover to serve what is happening in each scene. No. It does not work in opera. It is a rehearsal, not a workshop.

And also, musically it's not like symphonic music. Consider a performance of the Mahler Eighth. You have a single person – the conductor – standing in front of 200 musicians and that person's will must win the day. But in opera it's a far more collaborative operation among the orchestra, the conductor, the singers, the director, the designers. And as a working matter, you can't have just 'one will' being the sole focus. Some audiences get the impression that the *regisseur* has the 'one will'. That's just not true.

This is a problem specific to opera. And, unfortunately, I have worked with directors who think it'll be easy, that they'll get familiar with recordings of the piece and go into the rehearsal room and magic will ensue. What ends up happening is that they rely on their experienced singers to do what they, as directors, should have done. They become frustrated when things don't work out. Sometimes the results are funny; I worked with a guy once who was a very experienced stage director, working with a very famous and experienced cast, and he was trying to teach us how he wants a party scene to be. He talked and paused and stuttered and thought, and he just said, 'It should be 'OOOAHH!' And that was it. We had T-shirts made that said 'OOOAHH' and although we presented him with a T-shirt, I don't think he ever got the joke. Nice guy, though.

This is extreme. In truth, I have rarely worked with directors who simply had no idea what they wanted and were planning to rely on the rehearsal process to find out. More frequently I have dealt with directors who know what they want, but are inflexible about working with other people, or are overtly combative. And often they have too many ideas. When I was younger, a director came in and said to us at the first rehearsal, 'We all must realise that Wagner is no longer relevant'. I, being the performer of the lead role, said 'Then why are you here directing?'

I do speak back when somebody says something abjectly detrimental. As a singer, even a young singer, you have to know the boundaries. If it's about the work, fine. But if they start getting personal to you, or dismissive of you, or marginalising your work, then no. When I was in the national touring company of *Phantom of the Opera*, I asked one of the assistant directors why am I doing this thing here, and he said because that's the way they do it on Broadway. That's not direction. That doesn't support my work or the work of the team as a whole. That's narcissism.

You may assume that, because so many people seek the opportunity to direct a main show on the main stage of a major opera company, and there are so few opportunities, therefore the people who end up getting that gig – and a second and a third one – must reflect really good thinking. Preparing to stage a Wagner opera is not something you do while standing in a queue to pay for groceries. Yet many audience members leave the theatre with a sense that a particular director just didn't think it through – just didn't grapple with the challenges of the work and instead just slapped stuff up on the stage. That in some fundamental way they didn't engage with the work. Here's where I make the distinction.

I don't care whether a given production is modernised or a concept is being imposed on it or I'm being asked to wear a clown wig or to refer to a prop that is not there. Speaking now as a performer, not as an audience member, my rule is this: if I personally learn something new about a role – about my portrayal of a role – then I find it legitimate. And those are the directors I enjoy working with the most.

For example, I find Robert Carsen[1] a very, very, very fine stage director. A lot of people think of his stuff as too modern or too concept or too Eurotrash. But it's not. What he does is very thought-provoking and well thought-out. And with that one attribute – if it's really thought out – even some of the incongruities that may affect you become acceptable. A lot of the most established singers feel that way. Then it doesn't become about ego, like I don't do that, or they didn't ask enough for my input. It's not about that; it's about, did I learn something about this role that I didn't know before?

There is an exception. If it's contrary to the very ideas that are being expressed by the composer, then it's not legitimate. It happens in straight theatre; I saw a production of *The Hairy Ape*[2] by an *avant garde* group and sometimes the text was garbled but the raw, underlying emotions – the thing that the play was written in order to communicate – were palpable. So to me that production was legitimate. I didn't enjoy the production, but I received the primal rage that the text expressed. So I do think there is legitimacy in

---

[1] Carsen, born in Toronto in 1954, began his career in opera in 1979, when Lofti Mansouri, the director of the Canadian Opera Company, asked him to work as assistant director on a production of *Tristan und Isolde*. His Wagner productions since then have included a *Ring* Cycle for Cologne in 2000.
[2] A 1922 Expressionist play by the American playwright Eugene O'Neill (1888–1953).

pushing the envelope. But, again, it's easier to do that in straight theatre than in opera where the text and the composition are set.

There is a balance between time – the domain of the maestro – and space – the domain of the director. And those two domains have an artistic boundary between them. The director can't venture into choices of time. I've watched people try to stage something like the *Ring* and do so creating space that disrupts and interferes with the time. You don't say to a performer, jump on this trampoline and end up on this platform in time to sing your next line. That displays either ignorance or contempt for both the performer and the score.

This goes for the narrative as well as the visual. Each segment of the *Ring* needs to have coherence. There needs to be an arrow that goes in a linear way through all four of the stories. This has always been a problem with a sixteen-hour generational saga. Even the most prepared director would have difficulty keeping a linear thesis going, even with long rehearsal periods. Now, uniquely, there is such a thing as 'Workshop Bayreuth', and it can be remarkable the way it works. The way Patrice Chéreau re-staged Act III of *Walküre* over the five years of the run of his *Ring*.[3] Each year, the linear thread was made more clear until most believed it had always been such. What Herheim[4] did with his *Parsifal*. There is no director who is better prepared than Stefan Herheim when he comes to a first rehearsal. You may not agree with his concept, you may not agree with all of his ideas, but Herheim knows what he wants, when he wants it, and how he wants it. He has so many details; he is the consummate micromanager, controlling every detail that goes on. And for Bayreuth, even with that long rehearsal period for his *Parsifal*, it was sensational the first year, but you could see, there was so much he was trying to accomplish, with extras and crowds and costumes. The second year he was able to help the principals to flesh out their characters. And then in the third year it finally came together because

---

[3] Patrice Chéreau (1944–2013) – French director of theatre and opera, producer, filmmaker and actor – was entrusted with the '*Jahrhundertring*', the centenary production of *Der Ring des Nibelungen* at Bayreuth in 1976; it was conducted by Pierre Boulez, who had recommended him to the festival committee. Chéreau's staging set the *Ring* in Wagner's own time, emphasising nineteenth-century industrialism and hinting at a connection with fascism. It initially provoked much controversy, but its unity of direction, staging and lighting set a new standard, and after the final performance in 1980, it was hailed with a 45-minute standing ovation.

[4] The Wagner productions of Stefan Herheim, born in Oslo in 1970, began with *Tannhäuser* at the Landestheater Linz in 2001 and continued with *Das Rheingold* at the Latvian National Opera in Riga in 2006 (presented also at the Bergen Festival that year), *Parsifal* at Bayreuth in 2008, *Lohengrin* at the Deutsche Staatsoper in Berlin in 2009, *Tannhäuser* at the Norwegian National Opera in Oslo in 2010, *Die Meistersinger von Nürnberg*, a Salzburg/Opéra de la Bastille co-production in 2013, and *Die Walküre* and *Das Rheingold* at the Deutsche Staatsoper in Berlin in 2020 and 2021 respectively.

he finally had the time to put everything into a whole. And in the course of these revisions, he cut some things that didn't work; he's not proud in that sense. So there are some directors and some productions that will flourish in that environment. But if you're not prepared, if your concepts are not really fleshed-out, then you're not going to have a success, no matter how much time you have to rehearse.

On the musical side, you need similar sensitivity. I had the experience of working with a conductor who was absolutely the most mindlessly talentless conductor I'd ever encountered in my life. He was a technical musician; he had no sensitivity whatsoever. Compare with Gergiev, who is perhaps not technically as adept as many, but he has a musical sensitivity that finds a way to succeed for all involved.

A good conductor will reflect and accommodate the strengths and weaknesses of their singers. It is a defining attribute of Christian Thielemann and Zubin Mehta and James Levine and quite a few other great conductors, that they are the ones who take the time to learn who their singers are and accentuate their virtues and diminish their flaws. Zubin Mehta was my first 'angel', and he was there for every rehearsal, even piano rehearsals. For every production he had a private one-and-a-half-hour coaching session with every singer – whether they were young and new to the scene (as I was) or established giants, like Kurt Moll or Waltraud Meier, they all had a one-on-one with Zubin and a pianist. I was terrified the first time I was summoned; I thought I had done something wrong. The door opened and he was finishing up with Kurt Moll. Zubin just loves work, and he loves singers. Thielemann has never, ever left a singer in the lurch.

Say what you will about brilliant vocalists or conductors or stage interpreters; Wagner production works only if it is a complete collaboration. With stage directors you can roll with it. But with conductors, it's somewhat less flexible. When stars leave a production it's almost always because of the conductor. The relationship between the singers and the conductor is co-dependent, intimate, critical. If there is something you're being asked to do by the stage director that inhibits your ability to create the music, the conductor is the one who has the power to say 'No, have him do something different'.

And I must admit that the likelihood that I will learn something new about a role is much higher, usually, through a conductor's influence than a producer's. The exceptions aside, producers around the world are charged with creating what I would call a middle-line product that works day after day after day. They are hired to mount operas for audiences who love the operas they direct. In musical theatre, too, you sometimes see in lead roles on Broadway that many people don't stay there for more than a year or so,

VI: Working with Conductors and Stage Directors

in order to avoid the transformation from character to caricature. In opera as well, some people do a role 200, 300 times and they find they have fallen into reliance on *schtick*. That's why I think, especially in these heaviest and most profound of works, you have to have somebody who challenges you to look at the role in different ways.

I remember fondly the good training I had back in the New England Conservatory under John Moriarty's opera programme.[5] It was a very well-known programme for singers, and we would have 'arias for two'. They were short scenes where only one person was singing, but the other was reacting to what was happening, learning to stay alive and engaged in what was being sung. We had an aria class where you would take a small section of an aria and they would say sing it as if you were in a rage. Sing it as if you were singing it to the most beautiful woman or man you ever met. Changing emotions to see how it affects the colours or the event or the intent of the words. This taught me that even within the lines that were written, and were inflexible, there is an infinite variety of things you can do. That insight, in turn, makes me a more variable, more flexible artist. As I go from production to production, I can offer a broader artistic group of resources.

All of these considerations come into play when I'm working with a director like Tobias Kratzer,[6] who directed the *Tannhäuser* I've been doing in Bayreuth with the clown suit. At first people were taken aback because 'it's not what Wagner wrote': I'm not having sex with Venus and naked nymphs and satyrs aren't running around. But what did Wagner 'really write'? Tannhäuser leaves the constricting world of Wartburg where he could not tell the truth of life as he experiences it and dares to go outside convention. Kratzer won me over when he explained what we were: we were anarchists, a group of anarchists who had fled from society and abandoned social norms. Venus is the head, but she's kind of a demi-god. The dwarf, the drag queen and the despairing clown are running away and in battle with society, each for different reasons of their own. At the end of the story, and as the world of course always works, money rules – the dwarf is destitute, the drag queen has sold out, Tannhäuser is a broken man with no hope, and the only person in the group who has not changed, who is still doing her anarchist thing, is Venus. And that is because she is not a real person;

---

[5] As well as being a teacher of voice, John Moriarty (1930–2022) was also a conductor and producer of operas across the United States. He was also a good enough pianist to have studied with Egon Petri and a singer accomplished enough to have examined French vocal literature with Pierre Bernac.

[6] German stage-director (b. 1980), who directed the *Tannhäuser* that opened the Bayreuth Festival in 2019.

Four directors: clockwise from top left, Robert Carsen, Patrice Chéreau, Stefan Herheim and Tobias Kratzer

she is the personification of the subversive. That works for me, because it is exactly Wagner's point. Give me the clown outfit and let's have a go.

So you can change things and not have them fit exactly with the text but in so doing shed new light on a work we all care deeply about. Add to this an Elisabeth who is a really strong woman with an inner fragility that prompted her to attempt suicide when Tannhäuser left, and is extraordinarily angry when he comes back, but falls again helplessly under his spell and ends her own life when his life culminates in despair – this is good theatre. This is good stuff.

This, however, was relayed to us in an exciting manner as a concept that was holistic, that we could respond to, and that was coherent. You cannot accept a production concept, and interpretation of a great work, that is not holistically sensible. If a director is not prepared with a solid concept that can be understood and fortified in rehearsal, it simply will not take flight.

VI: Working with Conductors and Stage Directors

So let me try to put this in terms that I hope may be useful to the young artist building a career: With respect to the stage director, listen as hard as you can. Ask questions when you don't understand. Do the best you can. Some pushback is okay but look for opportunities to learn as much as you can. You're young and if things go well for you, this will be one of many, many times you will perform this role. By contrast, you stay with a bad conductor only until you are asked to hurt yourself or your work, and when that happens, do not back down.

VII
A Word on Technique

Vocal technique refers to a method of singing that you can safely and consistently, over a sustained period of time, replicate. It's that simple, and that basic.

No one wants to have a technique where their high C only happens sometimes, but not every time. Or sometimes I have a good *legato* line, but sometimes not. No. It's got to be a technique that makes it possible for you to concentrate on all the other aspects of the singing art – being onstage, acting, listening to other colleagues and responding to them, following the conductor and other musicians, phrasing, and doing all manner of stage business.

Many could be a Corelli,[1] if they went into a recording studio and lay down several takes of several phrases and then spliced them all together. There would be no worries if you could make twenty takes and then eventually find your high B flat with a *diminuendo*. But what made Corelli Corelli (at least in the first part and middle part of his career) was that he could go onstage and do all of this, every, every, every time. The minute you cannot recreate this effect, or it starts to go awry, then it's not a useful technique anymore.

The biggest challenge to a career boils down to this: capacity for repetition at the highest professional level over a sustained period. You must renew your own creative instincts again and again, while living with the voice in your body as it changes with time and circumstances.

It may be helpful if, at the outset, we consider the term *bel canto*, which is always spoken of with near-religious reverence. It has two meanings. As a technique it means the ability to string notes together in a *legato* line (the seeming uninterrupted progression of vowel tones) with control of amplitude variants of sound (that is, loudness), in a beautiful and consistent way. But the real meaning is one it has taken on, and that I use: a style rather than a technique. Everybody believes in *bel canto* if it means beautiful singing; but what does that mean? A sound that one person thinks is beautiful, another may not.

Take Wagner. He actually wrote that he intended his works to be sung 'in the Italian manner', which would have meant at the time *bel canto*, the tradition of Italian singing.

---

[1] Franco Corelli (1921–2003), Italian *spinto* tenor whose effortless technique led to his soubriquet of 'the prince of tenors'. He was a mainstay of the Metropolitan Opera from 1961 to 1975, although his career took him almost all of the major opera houses around the world.

Melodies, tunes, the stringing together of notes, the tone being consistent and lightly putting the text on top of that. But Wagner *bel canto* has to be put in the context of his text and how he wanted things to be declaimed. A different tone, or style, of singing can be just as beautiful as Italian. And even if it is not, a different style of singing is inevitable – it is dictated by the score and the vocal means to interpret that score.

What is '*bello*' in *bel canto* is, of course, both subjective (as each person has their own taste) and mutable (as tastes change). Remember that Rossini was appalled the first time he heard a tenor sing a high C with full modal (chest) voice, because tradition held that through the *passaggio*[2] and above G (for tenors) the notes maintained beauty only if produced in a pure head voice. For a very long time that was part of the Italian *bel canto* tradition. So when we get into the *verismo* period with Verdi and Puccini, it's still considered *bel canto* because it comes from that tradition, but what is considered beautiful, or perhaps unforced intensity, had changed from the early nineteenth century. The quality of the voice that we consider beautiful has evolved with time and repertoire.

So to define *bel canto* is impossible. It is a vocal method, a tradition, and it is also a style that is specific to a certain repertoire and a certain time-period. Therefore, whether it was *bel canto* that we heard in a performance last night in the opera house is extremely subjective. I heard an interview with Magda Olivero,[3] who had a very focused, beautiful, smaller voice. She was saying that, when doing recitative, she would keep the voice going past the tongue and the lips, in the front, and then just lightly speak though that constant tone and let the text 'fall' on the front of the lips. And that's kind of what recitative is, at least at the time of Mozart. And with a harpsicord or a light string accompaniment, you can do that. The voice will just sit at *mezza voce*[4] and speak through the *continuo*. And this not only makes it easier for the recitative to be more reflective of speech patterns, but also gives the artist more flexibility on where to emphasise certain words and where to pull back on certain tones.

We return to Wagner, who insisted that he was writing for singers to perform in the Italian style. But look at the score! With Wagner, you have a recitative style that he himself invented, that is a departure from the style associated with *bel canto*. It is very heavily scored, against a full-bodied and often very percussive orchestration. And as a performer you *have* to get the

---

[2] The transition area between vocal registers.
[3] Magda Olivero (1910–2014), born in Saluzzo, south-west of Turin, made her debut in 1932 and sang her last public performance in 1981. She had a distinguished career both before and after the Second World War, but her public profile was obscured by the 'battle' between Maria Callas and Renata Tebaldi.
[4] 'Medium' or 'half' voice.

VII: A Word on Technique

Franco Corelli and Magda Olivero

text out, with more propulsion, because you *have* to convey the narrative clearly. So at a minimum you have to provide more *vocale*,[5] simply to be heard at all. And once you do that, you have to apply five times sharper consonants. Think of it as a pressure washer – you have a constant volume of water coming through a tighter and tighter opening, so it ends up coming out with much more velocity and pressure. The same with singing, except that you're using air instead of water. The diaphragm must keep the pressure constant, the velocity under strict control, which is why it's so much more difficult to sing *piano* than *forte*.

This is important for people to understand: a Bellini singer or a Handel singer uses the same mechanism to produce the sound as the Wagner or Strauss singer. There is no difference in the diaphragmatic mechanism. In a way, every singer in every style of opera is on the stage because they can sing *bel canto*, in the sense that they can produce well-supported, flowing, uninterrupted, continual musical tone. That is objectively measurable. The question whether it is beautiful is entirely subjective, and that demonstrates the distinction between *bel canto* as a technique and *bel canto* as a style.

Sometimes comparisons can be helpful, so I'll make one up. On the one hand, you have Gould singing Siegfried. On the other hand, you have Mark Padmore singing the Evangelist in the *St Matthew Passion*. Both are considered top in their repertoire. They share a stream of constant melody, sound, *vocale*. They are both singing in the German language. Padmore has a solo cello or a keyboard under him; Gould has between 25 and 87 instruments under him. Gould uses his words differently from Padmore, because he has different conditions to come through the orchestration. But the basic mechanisms for singing are the same for both artists.

[5] The unobstructed and uninterrupted sound – vowel, as opposed to consonant.

But there is also a difference in our physical instruments. Gould has thicker, darker vocal mechanism, resulting in a sound whose focus and texture, timbre, flexibility and range are different from Padmore's. If you have thicker vocal folds, the result will sound different than if you have thinner ones. The resonance chambers that give feedback to the singer will be, from nature, different. One tenor will have higher overtones with a tighter *vibrato*[6] that is lighter and more brilliant. The other, a sound that is heavier or darker or more baritonal. The necessary balance between the focus (*squillo* or *squillando*[7]) and the column of air (open throat, raised soft palette) creates differences in timbre. And, indeed, I started out singing baritone roles for years. Our mechanisms are the same; the colour and the *timbre* of our voices are different.

There's a singer who was possessed of fabulous technique and musicianship. He also did a lot of contemporary scores that others couldn't or wouldn't sing. He had (by my ear) a phenomenally abrasive voice. You would hear him sing and think, this poor fellow, in three months, scraping his voice this way, he'll never last. Well, he had a 30-year career. His voice was powerful, it was interesting, it was well controlled, but it wasn't pretty. He could make it do anything he wanted, a range from low to high C without a problem. And he sang like this for 30 years. Opera houses hired him because he was a great actor, and he could sing pieces no one else could learn. By my definition of the term, this man had perfect technique. He produced his voice in a way that sometimes made you worry, but he could repeat that consistently and safely, night after night after night, without a problem. That is technique.

Let's pause here to make a side observation about the 'beauty' that some people think is implied in *bel canto* manner. In *Tannhäuser*, in the Act III Rome Narrative, my aim is not to make a series of 'beautiful' musical tones; it is to express the pain, suffering, despair, cynicism, the brokenness of the character. Wagner later wants you sing *legato*, of course, but at Tannhäuser's entrance Wagner writes: 'with a broken and destroyed voice'. There are plenty of opportunities where you can do some long, *legato* lines, but when you get to the parts that are hateful, and destructive, then you have to allow vocal colours (variants in the purity of tones) to express the text. I learned that not only from my own instinct, but from the conductor Franz Welser-Möst. He told me he liked the 'colours' I was putting in the Rome Narrative.

---

[6] A tightly controlled and constant change of pitch within the held note, that gives the tone a slight vibration.

[7] *Squillando*, often shortened to *squillo*, is a sharp, resonant quality of the voice that causes it to be heard through thick orchestration. It derives from the word describing sound of a trumpet and is sometimes described as a 'ping' – a brilliant ringing quality to the voice.

VII: A Word on Technique

We discussed it for a while, and he eventually said – on both our behalf, as we were discovering this simultaneously – yes, there are times when you have to dare to make ugly sounds.

A non-singer Wagner enthusiast may develop the impression that Wagnerian performers – Tristans and Siegfrieds – are hatched from rare eggs, that they have uniquely robust stamina, and so on. And they do. But Heldentenors are not hatched or even born. They are made. Heldentenor is an unnatural *Fach*. Wagner gave his singers different challenges than Bellini did but the challenges that are unique to each *Fach* are always there to overcome.

Perhaps earlier singers – in Mozart's time, or Handel's, or Donizetti's – had less radical choices to make; they were all expected to sing things a certain way. But Wagner invented something that was unfamiliar to contemporary audiences. Moreover, this development reflects changes in theatre itself. Culture evolves, and actors performing to audiences in Epidaurus in 250 BCE had different jobs than they did in the open-air Globe Theatre in 1601, or at the boisterous Haymarket in 1740 or doing Ibsen in a darkened auditorium in 1895 or at the experimental La Mama in 1963. Opera began with the Florentine *Camerata*, where singing was first used as a narrative tool in the 1570s. But from then to now is a comparatively short cultural history. *Castrati* had their opportunity to be creative and to thrill the audience in the final ornamentations at the end of arias. These were displays of pure vocalism, for vocalism's sake. The advent of recitative/aria structure gave way in Gluck's time to the aspiration for dramatic coherence. Then came Wagner and continuing through the period of twelve-tone composition, where in some cases text is more important than the tonality and melody of the score. All I'm saying is that things change, and the challenges of learned – acquired, trained – vocalism change with them.

Being a Heldentenor does not require 'special' technique, but it does require a voice that has certain attributes. These are not acquired – either you have them in your voice or else you sing other repertoire (if you are wise). There is a core sound that you need to have as a Heldentenor. I suspect that even non-singers know what they are. It has to be a sound that can cut through heavy orchestration. It has to be a sound that can articulate extreme consonants without clamping the voice. This means perfect coordination combined with a sizable amount of power. The heavier voices will be able to manage this against the orchestra better than the lighter voices. The lighter voices that achieve Heldentenor status all have an unusual ability to develop the *squillo*, the very high overtones, which have the greatest cutting effect. With time and maturity, power follows, the *timbre* darkens, and the technique can withstand Wagner's demands.

However, all Heldentenors will have to worry about the consistency of the vocal column against the consonant. If they chew the consonant too much, you end up getting the shouting, the 'Bayreuth bark', that people used to complain about. This happens because you're trying too hard to articulate the words, at the expense of the vocal undertone. (Pure vocal and muscular fatigue can also be a factor.) By the same token, if there is too much vocal undertone you lose the articulation. This is the problem: balance.

Stamina is one of the last qualities for a Wagner technique. Being a long-distance runner is much more important in Wagner than being a good sprinter. Wagner required a certain level of power, that more lyrical voices put themselves in danger of ruining their voices. The bigger voices, that can produce more sound, are in danger of producing a harsh, bark-y sound. Thus, a particular young artist might possess all the qualities from which one can build a perfect Wagnerian tenor; I can't think of an artist, however gifted, who did not require 'building' those qualities into a technique. Melchior is so often, and so correctly, cited as the perfect example. He had all the tools necessary to perform these roles, but these tools needed to be forged – he was, after all, a young baritone. Windgassen[8] is another example. He did not have as many of those tools as Melchior, but with time and patience and effort, and without pushing, he eventually got to the point where he could sing a large portion of the Wagnerian repertoire as a Heldentenor.

You will always sing within your own physiology. Each artist has a body and a chest and a set of vocal folds that define their sound. One is defined – and, perhaps, constrained – by one's gifts. That is not to say, however, that one might not discover, along the way, gifts that one didn't realise one had.

This happened to me while performing the *Ring* in Amsterdam. At that stage in my career I had begun singing a lot of Siegfrieds. I decided to re-work my technique while performing in the production of *Siegfried*, with my good friend and colleague Jan Hendrick Rootering.[9] He was singing Fafner in that production, and besides being one of the world's great

---

[8] The German Heldentenor Wolfgang Windgassen (1914–74) – son of another Heldentenor, Fritz Windgassen (1883–1963), and the coloratura soprano Vali von der Osten (1882–1923) – was a mainstay of the Staatsoper Stuttgart, where he succeeded his father as principal tenor. In 1951 he was invited to perform at the re-opening of the Bayreuth Festival, with Parsifal as his debut role. Between then and his last Bayreuth appearance in 1970, he sang all the important Wagnerian tenor roles: Erik, Loge, Lohengrin, both Siegfrieds, Siegmund, Tannhäuser, Tristan and Walther.

[9] Born in Germany in 1950, Rootering has appeared in opera in Hamburg and Munich, and other leading venues, including the role of the Landgrave at the Metropolitan Opera, Gurnemanz at the Opéra de la Bastille and Sachs at the Lyric Opera of Chicago..

VII: A Word on Technique

Wolfgang Windgassen and Jan Hendrick Rootering

helden-bass-baritones, he is also a great Wagnerian and vocal pedagogue. It was wonderful for me to work nearly every day with him during the three-month rehearsal period, and apply technical issues to the work at hand. I was getting very nasal in my singing because I was trying very hard to keep the 'point' in my voice at all costs. He directed me towards a balance. And suddenly the fullness of my voice started to come out, without so much nasality and stress. And the text was much more clear and focused. This was a watershed moment for me. It took fully a year before all of these aspects began to bloom in my voice. But that's what I mean when I say that you have to have natural ability – of course you do – but then it has to be built.

I've made a distinction between the long lines of *bel canto* and the strong percussive vocal production called for in certain roles. The former is simply safer for vocal health. I have to remind myself from time to time not to articulate too much. You can't do the long lines if you keep interrupting them with consonants. Italians can sing through their vowels without vocal interruption. In German it's much more problematic. One thinks that if you have the column of air going you can insert fricatives or plosives[10] at will. And I suppose that's true, or ought to be true. But it remains obvious to any performer that Lohengrin is more in the Italianate vocal tradition and that what Wagner wrote, for example, for Telramund or the young Siegfried is simply different. And this is because Wagner became increasingly interested in the words and epic poetry as a vital component of his work in performance. As you have to make crisper consonants, and as the consonants occur more rapidly, you need to lighten up the air in a

---

[10] The reference is to types of consonants. A 'fricative' is a sound caused by constriction of air-flow, and refers to sounds such as 'f' and 'th'. A 'plosive' is produced by stopping the air flow altogether and suddenly releasing it, such as 'k', 'g', 'p' and 'b'.

certain way. When this happens in a very intense moment it can lead to loss of presence. It is a natural temptation for singers to try to create this intensity through pushing.

Portamento[11] in Wagner is very rarely used today and, in essence, has a different approach. In Italian, during the *portamento* you are expected to hit every note on the way up and down. In German you go down much faster and emphasise the landing (a shorter period, more as a *glissando*[12]) – again, always on a strong consonant ending. Even this 'German style' of *portamento* is used sparingly, especially in Wagner's later works. So all of this can be seen broadly as, on the one hand, a focus on the sound and, on the other hand, a focus on the word.

When considering technique as an ever-evolving tool, two concerns arise: The first is misuse and injury, and the second is age.

Vocal injury can happen when you become too aggressive in the way you attack the breath and/or articulation. The great German baritone Franz Grundheber[13] is an example of perfect technique and articulation that gives him the ability to sing almost all music stylistically and is still doing so after 50 years on the stage. This is, again, what I mean by technique: the ability to replicate and renew one's skills over a long period of time. That is a true artist. Such artists do not allow themselves to start shouting the role.

Many Wagnerian roles, however, seem to be written to invite precisely that kind of misjudgement – or, put otherwise, to reward more prudent professional choices. The role of Ortrud in *Lohengrin* is written with enormous range of sound, but it is fluid. By contrast, Telramund is pounding; the singer needs to have a lot of aggression in his sound, and if you allow it to get into your technique, you will do yourself harm. You're putting pure aggression and pure pressure on your instrument. It's a very tiny little cartilage, after all, with tiny little muscles that can get tired. You allow it to tire and you're in trouble. There's going to be some of that, no matter what; nobody who sings Tristan with even the best technique should be doing any singing for many days thereafter. Another clean example is Mime shouting at Alberich in the second act of *Siegfried*. If you're an experienced character tenor, you can afford to make those sounds considering the short amount of time you have to do it. But you can't do that all night long, and that's what Telramund is expected to do.

---

[11] Sliding from one note to the other, as opposed to singing each with a distinct vocal attack – 'carrying' one note as the singer travels to the next one.
[12] Gliding from one pitch to another.
[13] Born in Trier in 1937, Grundheber joined the Hamburg Staatsoper in 1966 and performed over 150 roles there, in Italian as well as German repertoire.

VII: A Word on Technique   121

Franz Grundheber

Injury can also happen when early public success in your initial foray into the repertoire causes people whom you trust to encourage you to take on new roles quickly. This is the case of a tenor who, by his late thirties, is already singing the two Siegfrieds plus Tristan plus Tannhäuser. Or the young soprano doing Isolde and Brünnhilde and so on. That's imprudent and seldom leads to a career of 25 or 30 years.

Age, on the other hand, is not a misjudgement; it's an inevitability. As your body changes, your technique has to change, not only because of physical changes but because, over a career, audience tastes change. You have to adjust the way in which you make adjustments, if you see what I mean.

We all know many singers who had a kind of natural technique, who didn't know how they did what they did, or don't have to work so hard to train. And later in their careers they have a crisis and suddenly their careers are over, because there's nothing to fall back on. And as you age you have to accept that some things will simply go away. So you modify your technique just to get through what you have to do.

Opera singers are unlike actors in this respect: An actor, as they age, can go on to other roles that are appropriate to their age: A young man can go from Romeo to Hamlet to Macbeth to Othello to Lear. Opera roles stay, though. At 35 you may sing the young Siegfried. If you're lucky and you're still singing at 65, you're still singing the *Götterdämmerung* Siegfried. You can't move on to a role that is older or a different voice type. To paraphrase Gertrude Stein, a role is a role is a role.

Four mainstays of the Heldentenor tradition: clockwise from top left, Franz Völker, Sándor Kónya, Peter Seiffert and Klaus Florian Vogt

Not much of this age business is unique to Heldentenors. I do note however that, if (like me) you developed your career with a heavier voice – a voice that, in my case, came up from baritone – then your age will have an influence on your repertoire. That is to say, after a certain point you have to be careful of the roles you decide to continue to sing. Your repertoire will get smaller and smaller. This is because many of us can't go back to the lighter roles; I sang a lot of *Freischütz*es, a lot of *Fidelio*s in my younger days, where I could use the lighter *squillando* for power and for *legato*. You find that, after singing Siegfried – or really anything in the *Ring* – it gets harder and harder to go back to the other roles that are less challenging and more lyrical.

A lot of tenors save themselves by this balance – as they get older, they say that, for every *Siegfried* or *Walküre* that they sing, they'll do a series of

VII: A Word on Technique

*Freischütz*es or *Fidelio*s, or something that keeps some of the lyricism in the voice. My colleague Peter Seiffert[14] is not only one of the great Heldentenors, but one of the great tenors, period. He was very careful with his technique and his voice. He has sung everything at the highest international level, from Donizetti and Mozart all the way to Verdi and Wagner. But when he started singing the heavier roles, he always kept some of his Italian repertoire, some of his French repertoire. A few years ago he did a concert performance of *Fidelio* – and he's a few years older than I am – and I could tell he'd been working on his technique again because the performance was just flawless. Amazing. He was still singing some of the Italian *verismo* at that time. But he was capable of doing that because he came from the Italian *Fach* and built his voice slowly so that he could sing the heavier roles. Windgassen did that too. With me it's the exact opposite. At this point I can't really go back to that repertoire.

Also in the tradition of Franz Völker,[15] Sándor Kónya,[16] Wolfgang Windgassen and now Klaus Florian Vogt,[17] the great development of Heldentenors coming from the lyric *spinto* is assured.

So there may be a bit of an advantage to Heldentenors who came down from lighter roles because they can go back to these roles that are not as difficult, not as long. With us, who started with heavier, more baritonal foundations, it is more of a challenge to maintain these roles as we age.

---

[14] Born in Düsseldorf in 1954, Peter Seiffert studied at the Robert Schumann Hochschule there, joining first the Deutsche Oper am Rhein in his home city in 1978 and then the Deutsche Oper Berlin, where he remains. He first sang Erik there in 1980, adding Parsifal in London in 1988 and Lohengrin in Munich in 1989. In 1986 he married the Slovak soprano Lucia Popp (1939–93); after Popp's early death Seiffert married the Austrian soprano Petra-Maria Schnitzer (b. 1963), who herself has fine Wagner credentials.

[15] Franz Völker (1899–1965) made his debut (in Frankfurt, singing Florestan in *Fidelio*) at the age of only 27, and went on to become a stalwart of Salzburg, London and, especially, Bayreuth, from 1933; his Lohengrin was particularly esteemed. His prowess as a Wagnerian notwithstanding, he was equally at home in operetta and as a Lieder singer. His compliance with Nazi cultural policy closed non-German doors to him after the Second World War.

[16] The Hungarian tenor Sándor Kónya (1923–2002) first sang Lohengrin in Bayreuth in 1958, and the part soon became one of his signature roles: he sang it at the Paris Opera in 1959, La Scala in 1960, the Metropolitan Opera in 1961 and Covent Garden in 1963. His other Wagner roles included Erik in *Der fliegende Holländer* and Stolzing in *Die Meistersinger*.

[17] Born in Holstein in 1970, Klaus Florian Vogt began his musical career as a horn-player but put his instrument aside to study as a tenor, joining the company of Dresden Opera before turning freelance and is now hailed as one of the leading Wagner tenors of the day. He has sung Lohengrin at the Metropolitan Opera, La Scala, the Vienna State Opera and the Zurich Opera House, Tannhäuser at the Bavarian State Opera in Munich and Siegfried in a *Ring* cycle in Zurich. Since 2007 he has appeared at the Bayreuth Festival frequently, singing Lohengrin, Parsifal, Siegmund and Stolzing; Parsifal in particular he has sung in opera houses all around the world.

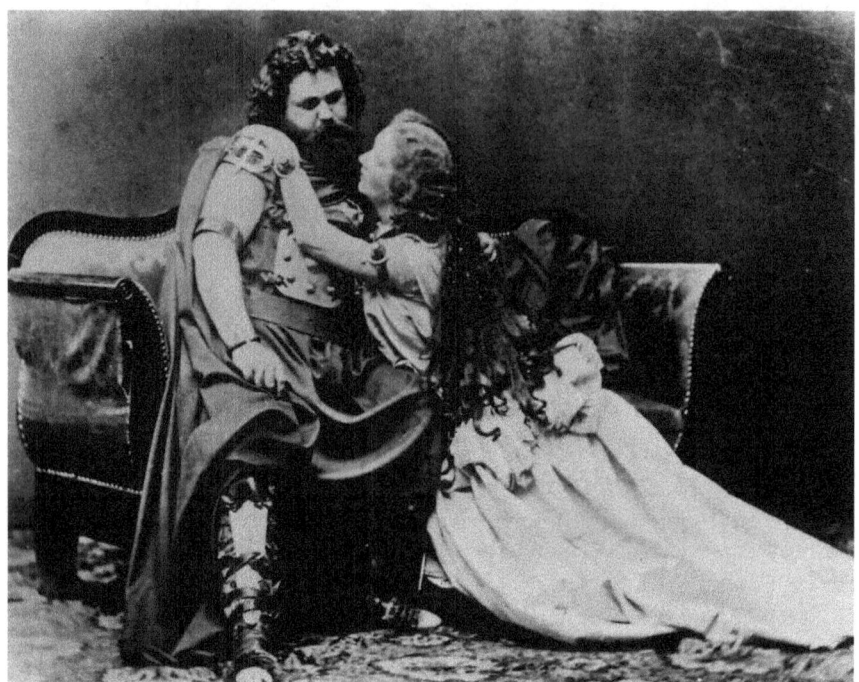

The short-lived Ludwig Schnorr von Carolsfeld and his wife Malwine in the title roles of the original production of Tristan und Isolde *in Munich in 1865*

I owe my success to my technique. Tannhäuser was the first Wagner role that I sang, and it's not usual that it happens. It wasn't even planned to happen. But it's because of the preparation in technique and stamina that my voice-teacher John Fiorito had instilled in me that made it possible for me to sing Tannhäuser for the first time. When you sing a mammoth piece for the first time, you're thinking first of your technique and second of your stamina – your ability to do a Shakespearean-length work like this where you're onstage the whole time. And traditionally, this particular role is recognised as one of the most difficult to sing. Some artists declined to essay it, for one reason or another (I suspect because, deep-down, they had doubts whether they could actually get through it). Of course, on a given night if you're not in absolutely perfect form, you do what you have to do to get it done. But the idea is, stop, let's calm down, let's not let the role take control of our technique.

All of this, by the way, allows us to better understand Wagner's constant search for performing artists for his works. He not only auditioned them – he *taught* them. And he aspired to an academy where singers would be taught a technique that existed in this balance between

VII: A Word on Technique

the lyrical sound and the cleanly articulated word. As I noted, Wagner specifically wrote his admiration for the Italian line. And at the same time, he wrote a note to the cast on opening night of the *Ring* to take care of the consonants (the words) because the vowels (the music) will take care of themselves. Watch for your technique, he said – give me clarity of performance and purity of tone. The ones who figured it out became the great Wagnerians and the ones who didn't, didn't.

Clearly his first Tristan got it. What Ludwig Schnorr von Carolsfeld[18] did with the words, his *squillando*, his power… When Wagner heard it, he just wept. And when von Carolsfeld died at the age of 29, Wagner despaired that he would ever find another tenor who could do the role. If only we – and others – could have heard it! Where would the ideal of Wagner singing be then? Nevertheless, I think that in the last twenty years we have had as fine practitioners as we have ever had.

Let me summarise with three broad concepts. First, there is a core technique of singing that all singers share and must have in order to have a career. Second, there are skills, techniques, that are learned and that mutate as your career is going on, ways to approach and overcome challenges as your body evolves. This is what I mean when I refer to technique as a way to successfully replicate your vocal performance over a series of occasions and a length of time. The third factor is how that relates to the public – what they accept and what they don't – and to conductors and coaches and the business of singing. It is not at all uncommon for a conductor to tell you that they want a certain something; it is your job as a singer to find a technical way to give them what they want.

In short: what is a Heldentenor? Answer: a tenor who successfully performs Wagner!

---

[18] *Cf.* note 1 on p. 35, above.

Epilogue
COLLEAGUES REMEMBER STEPHEN GOULD

Lise Davidsen

Wagner's *Tannhäuser* in Zürich, 2019, a Harry Kupfer production, conducted by Axel Kober – that was my first-ever time in the role of Elisabeth, and Stephen was singing the title role. I knew the name Stephen Gould, and his reputation was impressive, but I had never met him.

I remember being very nervous on my first day, as I often am with new roles. Above all, I'm scared to mess things up for members of the cast who have already done it many times before. During our run Stephen did his performance number 100 of the role, so he knew the opera inside out, and I was just beginning, with so much still to learn.

But there he was, a tall man with a big smile entering the rehearsal room. He carried his score in a tote-bag, and I remember thinking that he was so much more down to earth than I'd ever expected him to be. I also remember that he sang full voice. It became clear to me that he always had a couple more 'gears' for the performance, but that he very rarely marked in rehearsals. And that was one of the first things I learned from Stephen.

I had always felt that the only way for me to get on stage and feel comfortable with a role was to sing a lot in rehearsals, and to sing in full voice. That's the way I learn how to navigate a role, and to work out how much stamina is required – where I can give more, where I need to save some energy, and so on. And this is what Stephen did too, and seeing that from someone who had been in this industry for such a long time made me more sure of my thoughts, and more confident of what I had learned from my own experience.

And then there was the emotional aspect. Singing opera is very demanding. As an opera singer you leave your soul and heart on stage with every performance. And Stephen always did that. I could feel it and the audience could feel it. Even if something went wrong, or didn't go the way it had been planned – in the music or in the staging – he would still keep going. And yes, of course that's a given for professionals, but the way he did it was admirable. He gave it his all night after night, and that's something I will remember and take with me forever.

Stephen was not just down-to-earth; he was also admirably open. He was not the type of singer that would say: 'This is how it *should* be done'. He was open to how a production would be, and he did his best for the production and for all of his colleagues. Musically he was very open, too, complimenting his colleagues and not telling them, or me, what we did wrong. He knew and respected that everyone has their own process, and that we are all aware of what we are doing, and doing our best. If difficulties came up on stage we would work through them together, and try to find ways to help each other out. That respect for everyone, and staying open to different ways of doing things, is something I definitely learned from Stephen's example.

I will miss Stephen. We all will. And I wish that we had been able to work together many more times, over many more years. But every time I sing out in rehearsal, every time I renew my efforts to give my all on stage, regardless of obstacles or things that go awry, every time I strive to remain open to new possibilities and to collaborate with my colleagues to make the best of a production, and, yes, every time I carry my score in a tote-bag, I will remember him, and be grateful that I got to work with him, and to learn from him, as much as I did.

Markus Eiche

Our artistic collaboration spanned fifteen years of jointly rehearsing, devising and interpreting productions of the central operas of Richard Strauss and Richard Wagner, including *Tristan und Isolde*, *Tannhäuser*, *Götterdämmerung* and *Ariadne auf Naxos*. Over all these years we came together regularly for this work, and I always admired his irrepressible physical strength, which allowed him to deliver absolute vocal excellence in the heldentenor Fach at any time of the day or night, straight off the plane, with or without jetlag. I often asked him if he didn't want to take it easy for once, to which he always explained that he understood this unsparing attitude towards himself as training to keep himself vocally fit.

We had many and frequent discussions about how to find the most convincing artistic expression and how best to prepare for the purely vocal strain.

In this context, Stephen showed me an extremely effective vocal warmup exercise, which I am happy to share with you here. This exercise helps me a lot when I need to warm up my voice very quickly or when I am looking for vocal recovery from a stressful phrase.

Stephen Gould's Singing 'Overblow Exercise'
- Blow air through your almost closed lips with thick cheek pouches.
- Repeat for each new breath and
- Also play with the pressure of the teeth on each other.
- Ask yourself, What is the tongue doing?

- Decide on a free, channelling position of the tongue with the jaw slightly open.
- When you have a feeling that the energy for the steady flow of air is coming from deep in your body, add your head voice.
- Then, with repeated breaths, try various *glissandi* over the whole range of your head voice accompanied by the blowing sound of the lips with the cheek pouches fully distended.

Thank you, Stephen, for the wonderful hours together on and off stage! I told you we would miss you, and now we do!

Catherine Foster

I am deeply touched to have been invited to write about my experiences with Stephen Gould. I have written many versions of this text and scrapped even more, since writing a simple paragraph on such an extraordinary singer, colleague and friend is just not possible. So I will do my best.

I first sang with Stephen in 2006, as a very new singer to the stage and my first big guesting job, at the Dresden Semper Oper, he was Kaiser to my Kaiserin.[1] After that we sang together many times as Siegfried and Brünnhilde, Tristan and Isolde and even Elektra and Aegisth. His approach to singing was always unique and deeply moving. He embodied the very character he was singing, which showed me the way many times to delve deeper into my characters, and I felt that uniqueness of being on stage not as two people but as one. He was always so generous in that way.

In 2022 I had the gift of coming together to sing *Tristan* with him for the first time and on the Bayreuth stage – a unique experience in itself from the acoustics to the history that is in the very building. I began studying and singing Isolde in 2011, with a gap of several years: I chose not to sing her again until 2019, since it is a role that requires the deepest respect, the best of techniques and a willingness to let go of everything you thought you knew. This evaluation only deepens the longer you sing the role! With Stephen he took this approach onto another level again: his insights, his voice and his understanding of the role helped me again to move towards an Isolde that is simply to be experienced, simply to be, and to finally let go of the

---

[1] In Richard Strauss' *Die Frau ohne Schatten*. —ED.

'why's and 'what if's. After all, *Tristan und Isolde* is all about transcendence, I remember him saying during one rehearsal.

In June 2023 during the rehearsals of *Tristan und Isolde* in Bayreuth again, we came together to sing the Orchestral *Sitzprobe* in the restaurant. It was there that I really knew something wasn't right and that Stephen would not be doing the shows, but it was his wish to sing 'one last time' with the Bayreuth Orchestra. He apologised to me for this, to which I simply replied: 'Who cares? You've earned it, so let's just sing and make music!' I will always hold dear that experience of singing Tristan side by side in the restaurant. We were as one singing together and letting the music of *Tristan und Isolde* simply flow through us. He sounded as glorious and passionate as he ever had before.

Ekaterina Gubanova

It is not easy to write about Stephen and to avoid praise. I'm so very grateful that I got to work with him quite a lot. For me Stephen was an incredible combination of qualities that you rarely find in one artist (or person, for that matter!). Apart from the voice like no other, he was insanely perfect with all the musical details. I remember the first music call of *Tannhäuser* in Dresden. I could not believe my own ears. You don't expect such refinement from this type of voice. He was doing seemingly impossible dynamics and colours – bending this mountain of a voice to his will (and the will of Wagner).

And then comes his profound knowledge of the material: Stephen was practically teaching the young conductor by executing everything that is written in the score, to the smallest detail. And we know that when it comes to Wagner, there will be about 168 things that a singer should do in just one bar! Since it was my first time singing with Stephen, my jaw just dropped.

Knowing how much work goes into achieving these results, you'd expect a very serious person, perhaps even uptight. And instead you got a very easy going, supportive colleague, who (once you know each other a bit better) was always ready to have fun! He had this certain twinkle in his eye that could make you laugh before he even said anything!

Stephen was also incredibly graceful, despite of his absolute star status. I have seen far less deserving 'stars' taking it out on staff and colleagues.

There is a gaping hole in the Wagnerian world now that Stephen is gone. No other tenor these days has this sheer power and nobility of tone. And of course Bayreuth is particularly orphaned…. We will miss you so much, dear Stephen.

Tomasz Konieczny

I met Stephen Gould during my first production at the Vienna State Opera. The then director Ioan Holländer hired Stephen for the role of Siegfried and me as Alberich in the newly created *Der Ring des Nibelungen*, directed by Sven-Erich Bechtolf and under the musical direction of Franz Welser-Möst. It was 2008, I was a little-known singer, a debutant in Vienna, just starting his adventure with the music of Richard Wagner. As it turned out later, I was on the threshold of an international singing career.

Stephen was an older colleague whom I stared at like a picture. I remember Siegfried's dress rehearsal, which began, as is often the case at the Wiener Staastsoper, as early as 10:00 (Strauss' *Salome* was being performed in the evening of that same day) and the absolute professionalism of Stephen, who due to the inhuman time of the dress rehearsal had to appear in the make-up of that day as early as 8:00, which is quite a challenge for a singer, especially a Wagnerist. But Stephen also sounded and presented his heroic role fantastically.

He was always a great authority for me. Stephen was the colleague who helped me a lot when, after three years of singing the Alberich part, I 'switched' to my life and target part of Wotan at the Wiener Staatsoper. Although many people were sceptical about this switch of roles, from the beginning Stephen believed in me very much and supported my actions. He helped me during rehearsals, he respected me. I have the impression that he liked me.

I remember his wonderful interpretation of Erik in *Der fliegende Holländer* at the Vienna State Opera, in a difficult staging by Christine Mielitz. I was in the audience. I flew to Stephen's dressing room after the show to tell him that he was the best Erik in the world. It was a truly remarkable interpretation of this tenor role, one which is not always liked.

For the last time on stage, and in fact on the concert podium, I met Stephen during the pandemic in Tokyo. All the singers were then forced to quarantine for ten days in the hotel where we were staying. We talked a lot. Stephen told me about his journey, about his love for Wagner's music theatre, about Bayreuth, where he felt at home. He talked about Wolfgang Wagner, who was like a father to him. Stephen loved sushi, which was eagerly used by Japanese partners, including the organiser of the Tokyo Spring Festival, Mr Suzuki. During concert tours in Japan, we were often invited to exclusive dinners, basically demonstrations of preparing sushi and other Asian delicacies. Those were great moments to look forward to – and back on.

Stephen was one of those great Wagnerian and Straussian giant tenors. He was a beautiful artist and a great colleague. He left much too early. I will miss him very much. R.I.P., dear Stephen.

Petra Lang

I knew Stephen Gould from 2005, and loved his direct approach to his own singing and to life and the way he therefore dealt with singers, conductors and circumstances in the business. He was always an affable, helpful and supportive colleague and a friendly person. Together we sang Mahler's Eighth Symphony in Paris and Budapest, *Ariadne auf Naxos* at the Semper Oper in Dresden, *Götterdämmerung* in Munich and Tokyo, *Tristan und Isolde* in Bayreuth and Munich and at the Vienna State Opera. In many conversations I had with Stephen during and between rehearsals, I was able to extract the following for myself from his attitude:

1. *As a singer, you really have to know what you are doing singing-wise.*
2. *Warming-up is important!* Falsetto exercises help tenors 'warm up' the voice.
3. *You have to put the voice into the mask and 'feed' the place permanently.* Otherwise you might not have a professional career; maybe you will make it for one or two years 'in agony' in small theatres, if you cannot project your voice.
4. *Singing is individual!* Accept your body and your voice and always work on optimizing the way you use them. You need to find and feel your projection of your voice, know how and when to use it. Find your stamina with your flexibility.

5. *Accept that it takes time for the voice to 'find its way'.* No master has fallen from the sky yet. 'Crises' are part of the path. That's how you learn to distinguish wrong from right.

6. *You learn your roles properly only on stage.* Trust that you will meet the right people at the right time who will help you in your development as a singer. This also takes courage on the part of the organisers, conductors, stage directors, who recognise your potential, believe in you and give you a chance.

7. *If you really have to sing, you will do anything to get into the profession.* For example, you drive a cab at night for night pay, you do physically hard work, and you take any singing job across genres that will help you build your stamina and further your vocal development.

8. *To sing the German repertoire, you must really speak the German language.* If you want to sing Wagner, you must have a very good command of the German language. Find a place to live in a country where German is spoken. Working out the roles with coaches is not enough. To really get through the parts, you must understand the text and be able to 'think' the character in German.

9. *Believe in your destiny and pursue your goal.* Be persistent.

10. *Be brave!* Sometimes as a singer you have to jump in at the deep end. This takes courage. Courage comes from your years of intense preparation, never losing sight of your goal.

11. *Pass on your knowledge and experience to young singers.* They must learn to define *their* goals, to be able to evaluate the path and decide if this is really *their* path. To do this, they must learn how to accomplish the path. Be generous in sharing your knowledge. Singers have shown you their secrets. If you can afford it: then it's payback day.

12. *Never take criticism personally.*

Tichina Vaughn

I met Stephen Gould as his Venus in the opera *Tannhäuser*. Though I had previously performed the role in other opera houses, this production was special as it represented a bundle of debuts. It was my debut season as a member of the ensemble of the world-renowned Semper Oper in Dresden, my Wagnerian debut in the opera house where Wagner himself was Kapellmeister (and, in fact, premiered *Tannhäuser*), as well as my role debut for an East German public. Though not generally one to suffer from anxious thoughts, I can now admit to experiencing a few back then.

From our first meeting, Stephen's confident demeanour and generous work-ethic encouraged me to remember that we do not perform for specific audiences or regions, but in service to the work at hand. His mastery of the material and gracious nature drew us into an artistic work-space where I was able to focus on our artistic aims and dismiss unfounded doubts and inhibitions.

Having such a gifted and experienced colleague who was also a countryman was an unquestionable asset in this situation. I was more than grateful for his presence and prowess.

These were our only shared performances. However, they were important and memorable for me, since the entire experience reminded me to be about the work and to occupy fully whatever space it allows you to inhabit. That lesson came at the beginning of many successful years at the Semper Oper, and continues to be profitable till the present day.

Michael Volle

I always looked forward very much to meeting Stephen again and to be on stage with him (which is not the same with all colleagues), because his friendliness was always catching, and his absolutely professional behaviour such a good example.

Singing his first note, he was totally inside his role – even if he had to fight with a lot of sometimes weird stagings. And I know by my own experiences how difficult this can be – only if you accept whatever kind of 'surroundings' you may have will you be able to sing as well as possible.

And to this he was always committed.

Discography

BEETHOVEN
Symphony No. 9 in D minor, Op. 125
Elizabeth Bishop, Mary Dunleavy, Stephen Gould, Alastair Miles; Atlanta Symphony Orchestra and Chorus; Donald Runnicles, conductor
Telarc CD-80603 (CD; 2003)

KORNGOLD
Prayer, Op. 32
Album: Music from *Much Ado about Nothing, Abschiedslieder, Einfache Lieder, Tomorrow, Prayer*
Gigi Mitchell-Velaso, Stephen Gould; Ladies of The Mozart Choir, Linz; Bruckner Orchester Linz; Caspar Richter, conductor
ASV CDDCA1131 (CD; 2002)

SCHOENBERG
Gurre-Lieder
Stephen Gould (Waldemar), Camilla Nylund (Tove), Christa Mayer (Waldtaube), Markus Marquardt (Bauer), Wolfgang Ablinger-Sperrhacke (Klaus-Narr), Franz Grundheber (Speaker); MDR Leipzig Radio Choir, Saxon State Opera Choir Dresden, Gustav Mahler Youth Orchestra, Staatskapelle Dresden; Christian Thielemann, conductor
Profil Edition Günter Hänssler PH20052 (2 CDs; 2020)

RICHARD STRAUSS
Die Frau ohne Schatten
Stephen Gould (The Emperor), Anne Schwanewilms (The Empress), Michaela Schuster (The Nurse), Wolfgang Koch (Barak the Dyer); Evelyn Herlitzius (Barak's Wife); Vienna Philharmonic, Salzburg Festival; Christian Thielemann, conductor
Opus Arte OABD7104D (DVD/Blu-Ray; 2012)

Die Frau ohne Schatten
Stephen Gould (The Emperor), Camilla Nylund (The Empress), Evelyn Herlitzius (The Nurse), Wolfgang Koch (Barak the Dyer), Nina Stemme (Dyer's Wife); Vienna State Opera Orchestra; Christian Thielemann, conductor
Orfeo C991203 (3 CDs; 2020)

RICHARD WAGNER

Götterdämmerung
Stephen Gould (Siegfried), Linda Watson (Brünnhilde), Ralf Lukas (Gunther), Andrew Shore (Alberich), Hans-Peter König (Hagen), Edith Haller (Gutrune/Third Norn), Christa Mayer (Waltraute), Fionnuala McCarthy (Woglinde), Ulrike Helzel (Wellgunde), Simone Schröder (Flosshilde/First Norn), Martina Dike (Second Norn); Bayreuth Festival Orchestra and Chorus; Christian Thielemann, conductor
Opus Arte OACD9004D (4 CDs; 2010)

Götterdämmerung
Stephen Gould (Siegfried), Linda Watson (Brünnhilde), Markus Eiche (Gunther), Tomasz Konieczny (Alberich), Attila Jun (Hagen), Caroline Wenborne (Gutrune), Janina Baechle (Waltraute), Ileana Tonca (Woglinde), Zoryana Kushpler (First Norn/Flosshilde), Ulrike Helzel (Second Norn/Wellgunde), Ildikò Raimondi (Third Norn); Vienna State Opera Orchestra and Chorus; Christian Thielemann, conductor
Deutsche Grammophon 4791830 (4 CDs, 2013)

Parsifal
Michael Volle (Amfortas), Ryan Speedo Green (Titurel), Falk Struckmann (Gurnemanz), Stephen Gould (Parsifal), Boaz Daniel (Klingsor), Violeta Urmana (Kundry); Vienna State Opera Orchestra and Chorus; Ádám Fischer, conductor
Vienna Staatsoper (streaming at https://www.operaonvideo.com/parsifal-vienna-2016-gould-urmana-volle-struckmann-daniel/; 2016)

Siegfried
Stephen Gould (Siegfried), Gerhard Siegel (Mime), Albert Dohmen (Der Wanderer), Andrew Shore (Alberich), Hans-Peter König (Fafner), Linda Watson (Brünnhilde), Christa Mayer (Erda), Robin Johannsen (Waldvogel); Bayreuth Festival Orchestra and Chorus; Christian Thielemann, conductor
Opus Arte OACD9003D (4 CDs; 2010)

Siegfried
Stephen Gould (Siegfried), Christian Elsner (Mime), Tomasz Konieczny (Der Wanderer/Wotan), Jochen Schmeckenbecher (Alberich), Matti Salminen (Fafner), Violeta Urmana (Brünnhilde), Anna Larsson (Erda), Sophie Klussmann (Waldvogel); Rundfunk-Sinfonieorchester Berlin; Marek Janowski, conductor
Pentatone PTC5186408 (3 SACDs; 2013)

Tannhäuser
Stephen Gould (Tannhäuser), Lise Davidsen (Elisabeth), Elena Zhidkova (Venus), Markus Eiche (Wolfram von Eschenbach), Stephen Milling (Hermann); Bayreuth Festival Orchestra and Chorus; Valéry Gergiev, conductor
Deutsche Grammophon DG 735 757 (DVD/Blu-Ray; 2020)

Discography

Tristan und Isolde
Stephen Gould (Tristan), Nina Stemme (Isolde), Kwangchul Youn (König Marke), Johan Reuter (Kurwenal), Michelle Breedt (Brangäne), Simon Pauly (Melot), Clemens Bieber (A Shepherd), Arttu Kataja (Steersman), Timothy Fallon (Young Sailor); Rundfunk-Sinfonieorchester Berlin; Marek Janowski, conductor
Pentatone PTC5186404 (3 CDs; 2012)

Tristan und Isolde
Stephen Gould (Tristan), Evelyn Herlitzius (Isolde), Georg Zeppenfeld (König Marke), Iain Paterson (Kurwenal), Christa Mayer (Brangäne), Raimund Nolte (Melot), Tansel Akzeybek (A Shepherd/Young Sailor), Kay Stiefermann (Steersman), Bayreuth Festival Orchestra and Chorus; Christian Thielemann, conductor
Deutsche Grammophon DG 073 5251 (2 DVDs/Blu-Rays; 2015)

Index of Operas and Operatic Roles

page numbers in italics indicate an illustration;
SG = Stephen Gould

A: WAGNER

Alberich (*The Ring*), 51, 53, 54, 94, 120, 136
Amfortas (*Parsifal*), 94, 95, *96*, 98

Brangäne (*Tristan und Isolde*), 39, 46n
Brünnhilde (*The Ring*), 9, 40, 46n, 62, 65–66, 121, 133

Dutchman (*Der fliegende Holländer*), 82n, 83

Elisabeth (*Tannhäuser*), 19, 46n, 108, 129
Elsa (*Lohengrin*), 82, 84
Erik (*Der fliegende Holländer*), 7, 9, 82–86, 118n, 123n, 137
   cabaletta, 82–83

Fafner (*The Ring*), 53–54, 56, 63, 66, 73
Fasolt (*The Ring*), 53–54
fliegende Holländer, Der, 64n, 80, 81, 82–83
   at Bayrische Staatsoper (2012), 82n
   at Wiener Staatsoper, 137
Flosshilde (*The Ring*), 75
Freia (*The Ring*), 45n, 51, 52
Fricka (*The Ring*), 46n, 52, 56
Froh (*The Ring*), 74

Gibichungs (*The Ring*), 69–70
Götterdämmerung, 9, 40, 57, 62, 67, 121, 131, 138
   flaws in the narrative, 69, 70
Grane (*The Ring*), 70
Gunther (*The Ring*), 70–73
Gurnemanz (*Parsifal*), 89, 93, 95, 118n
Gutrune (*The Ring*), 70–72

Heinrich (*Der fliegende Holländer*), 84
Hagen (*The Ring*), 70–72, 74

Isolde (*Tristan und Isolde*), 33–48, *41*, 46, 121, 133

Klingsor (*Parsifal*), 93–94
Kundry (*Parsifal*), 43n, 46n, 91, 93, 94, *96*
Kurwenal (*Tristan*), 39, 44

Landgrave (*Tannhäuser*), 17–19, 27, 118n
Loge (*The Ring*), 9, 51–55, 61n, 64, 65, 118n
   his dual character, 52–53
   a *Heldentenor* role, 53, 55
   in *Götterdämmerung*, 54
   his relationship with the audience, 54–55
   the most interesting character in the *Ring*, 54
   SG's enjoyment of the role, 55
   tessitura, 57
Lohengrin, 79–86, 120
   at Bayreuth (2021), 82
   in Hamburg (1988), 84
   in Berlin (2009), 105n
   musical strength and dramatic weakness, 79, 81–82
   as part of Wagner's development, 80–81
   Act III mirroring Wagner's own life, 81–82
   absurdity of the plot, 83–84
Lohengrin (the role), 7, 9, 43n, 53, 61n, 75, 79–86, *85*, 98, 118n, 119, 123n
   balance with the orchestra, 81
   weak characterisation, 79–80
   SG trying to make sense of the role, 83–86

Marke (*Tristan und Isolde*), 39, 40, 42–44, 47
Meistersinger, Die, 81, 105n, 123n
Melot (*Tristan und Isolde*), 39, 42–44
Mime (*The Ring*), 59, 61, 61n, 62, 66, 67, 69, 74, 120

147

Norns (*The Ring*), 68, 74

Ortrud (*Lohengrin*), 46n, 80, 120
Oskar (silent role in *Tannhäuser*), *29–30*

Parsifal, 37, 45, 46n, 58, 89–98, 105
   in Graz (2003), 90
   in Bayreuth (2008), 105n
   concert performance in Bayreuth (2021), 91
   the epitome of Wagner's mature style, 89–90
   Christian philosophy, 92, 93, 98
   the Grail, 92, 93, 98
   Schopenhauer, 92
   Buddhism, 91–92, 94
   Klingsor's *Zaubergarten* (Magic Garden), 93
   Parsifal's journey, 93–94
   the pivotal moment in the drama, 94
   Act III as dénouement, 94–95
   Karfreitag (Good Friday), 95
   Parsifal and redemption, 98
   Parsifal (the role), 7, 9, 57n, 61n, 89–98, *96*, 118n, 123n
   the *reine Tor*, 89, 92
   the age of Parsifal, 89
   Parsifal like a Shakespeare fool, 89
   the nature of the role vocally, 90
   the character hard for an audience to follow, 91
   SG's experience of singing the role, 90–91
   the experience of the concert performance in Bayreuth (2021)
   Parsifal's journey, 93
   the rejection of Kundry, 95
   the power of *Mitleid*, 95

Rheingold, Das
   in Riga (2006), 105n
   in Berlin (2021), 105n
   its place in the *Ring*, 51–52
Rhinemaidens (*The Ring*), 74
Rienzi, 80
Ring des Nibelungen, Der (the *Ring* cycle), 9, 81, 90, 122, 136
   performed for the first time in China, 46n
   at Metropolitan Opera, New York (1989), 52–53
   at Covent Garden, London, 55n
   at Finnish National Opera, Helsinki, 55n

   at Bayreuth (1988), 64n
   in Cologne (2000), 104n
   in Amsterdam, 118
   in Zurich, 123n
   the centenary production at Bayreuth (1976), 105n
   tessitura of tenor roles in the *Ring*, 57
   Wagner and the 'new art', 60
   the Tarnhelm, 74
   the coherence of the cycle, 105

Sachs (*Die Meistersinger*), 118n
Senta (*Der fliegende Holländer*), 64n, 82–83
Siegfried, 9, 118, 120, 122
   Forest scene, 9
   Forging scene, 9
   opening scene, 60–61
   Wagner's change of direction in *Siegfried*, 65
   Act III, 68
Siegfried (the role), 7, 9, 12, 36, *71*, 80, 84, 92, 115, 117, 118n, 119, 121, 122, 133, 136
   the role in *Siegfried*, 59–67
   tessitura, 57
   entrance with a bear, 59
   singing what is written, 59
   Siegfried's childhood, 60
   technical challenge for a singer, 60–61
   Siegfried as 'nature child', 61–62
   hatred of Mime, 62
   the sword, 63
   meeting Wotan, 63
   the *Neidhöhle*, 63
   meeting Wotan (the Wanderer), 65
   the challenge of the final scene, 66
   awaking Brünnhilde, 66–67
   the role in *Götterdämmerung*, 68–76
   Siegfried in *Götterdämmerung* not making sense, 68
   the Rhine journey, 69, 72
   relationship with Brünnhilde, 69–73
   the opening duet, 70
   the potion, 70–72, 74
   Nothung, 72
   the ring, 73–74
   Siegfried's deceit, 73
   Siegfried and fear, 75
   Siegfried in *Götterdämmerung* the 'least well-written of Wagner's characters', 75–76
Sieglinde (*The Ring*), 43n, 46n, 56–58, 62

Index of Operas and Operatic Roles   149

Siegmund (*The Ring*), 7, 9, 53, 56–58, 74,
  86, 89, 118n, 123n
  as a hero and doomed character, 56
  compared to Siegfried, 56–57
  the 'Wälse' cries, 57
  the least satisfying of the tenor roles in
    the *Ring*, 57
  the *Todesverkündigung* (Act II of *Die
    Walküre*), 58
  Siegmund and self-sacrifice, 58
Stolzing (*Die Meistersinger*), 123n

Tannhäuser, 15–32, 61, 131
  in Bayreuth (2022), *22, 25, 29, 30*, 101
  in Dresden (2010), *26*
  at Bayreuth (1972), 55n
  at Bayreuth (2019), 107
  in Linz (2001), 105n
  in Oslo (2010), 105n
  in Zurich (2019), 219
  premiere in Dresden, 140
  Act III and Tannhäuser's despair, 28
  and Catholicism, 17, 21, 27
  the chorus, 24-26
  Christian references, 17, 19
  historical Tannhäuser, *18*, 19n
  historical Elisabeth, 19n
  the very first version, 28n
  Paris version, 27, 27n
  the Pope, 21, 27–28, 31
  premiere (1845), *20*, 27n
  redemption, 23, 27–28
  religious implications, 17
  salvation through a woman, 28–31
  spiritual exploration, 17
  the song contest, 21, 24–26
  the Venusberg, 17–23, 28
  Venusberg Bacchanale, 27n
  the Virgin Mary, 19, 21, 23
  the Wartburg, 19, 19n, 23, 24, 28
  journey to Rome, 23, 27–28, 31, 116–17
  Tannhäuser (the role), 7, 9, 12, 13, *20,
    22, 25, 26*, 61, 90, 108, 118n, 121,
    123n, 124, 129, 135
  how the singer copes while waiting in
    the wings, 21–23
  as minnesinger, 23–24
  motivation, 17–19, 27
  leaving Venus, 23, 24
  relationship with Elisabeth, 19–21, 23,
    24, 26–28
  and the song contest, 24
  his motivation, 17–18

  the outsider pitted against society, 17
  the demands of the role, 124
Telramund (*Lohengrin*), 80, 119
Titurel (*Parsifal*), 95
Tristan und Isolde, 7, 17, 19, 31, 33–48, 81,
  89, 90, 131, 138
  in Bayreuth (2018), 40, 44
  in London, 45
  in Munich, (1998), 43n, 44
  in Bayreuth (2015), 46n
  in Canada, 104n
  in Bayreuth (2022), 133
  in Bayreuth (2023), 133
  first performances, 35, 35n, *124*
  the 'mystical, mythical experience' of
    Tristan, 35
  challenges of the musical style, 36
  emotion rather than narrative, 35–39
  a 'symphony of souls', 46
  Tristan and Schopenhauer, 37
  the words, 38
  Tristan inviting death, 38–39
  journey through love towards death, 39
  the love potion, 40
  Act I, 39–41
  Act II, 42–44
  Act III, 44–45
  the three narratives of Act III, 44–45
  Tristan (the role), 7, 9, 12, *41, 42*, 43n,
    47, 61n, 69, 84, 90, 98, 117, 118, 120,
    121, 133
  the first Tristan, 35, *124*, 125
  SG learning the role, 36
  SG's immersion in the role, 36–38, 45,
    46
  Tristram in legend, 38
  Tristan as Tantris, 39, 40
  the confrontation with Marke, 43–44
  the death of Tristan, 44–45

Venus (*Tannhäuser*), 17, *20*, 21, 23, 24, *26*,
  28, *30*, 46n, 107–8

Walküre, Die, 63, 105, 122
  at Bayreuth (2000), 43n
  in Berlin (2020)
Walther (*Die Meistersinger*), 118n
Waltraute (*The Ring*), 46, 54
Wellgunde (*The Ring*), 75
Woglinde (*The Ring*), 75
Wolfram (*Tannhäuser*), 24, 28
Woodbird (*Siegfried*), 63–64, 74

Wotan (The *Ring*), 13, 51–54, 56, 58, 63, 64–65, 67, 75, 94, 136

B: OTHER COMPOSERS
Aegisth (Richard Strauss, *Elektra*), 133
Ariadne auf Naxos (Richard Strauss), 131, 138
Bacchus (Richard Strauss, *Ariadne auf Naxos*), 7

Don Ottavio (Mozart, *Don Giovanni*), 82

Elektra (*Elektra*), 133

Fidelio (Beethoven), 122–23, 123n
Florestan (Beethoven, *Fidelio*), 7, 123n
Freischütz, Der (Weber), 122–23

Jenůfa (Janáček), 55n

Kaiser (Richard Strauss, *Die Frau ohne Schatten*), 7, 133
Kaiserin (Richard Strauss, *Die Frau ohne Schatten*), 133

Paul (Korngold, *Die tote Stadt*), 7
Peter Grimes (Britten, *Peter Grimes*), 17

Otello (Verdi, *Otello*), 7, 66

Salome (Richard Strauss), 136

Turn of the Screw, The (Britten), 64n

General Index

Anda, Alois, 35n
Anderson, Martin, 13
Antwerp, 83
Arens, Uwe, 13
Arthurian legend, 38
avatars, 98

Baby Huey, 61
Baden-Baden
    SG as Parsifal there, 91
Bayreuth, 7, 9, 10, 12, 29, 36, 43n, 45n, 46n, 61, 61n, 64n, 90, 91, 105, 105n, 123n, 137, 138
'Bayreuth bark', 118
Bayreuth Festival, 7, 13, 90n, 123n
    re-opening in 1924, 57n
    re-opening in 1951, 118n
    2008, 46n
    2020 (cancelled), 91
    2021, 91
    2022, *22*n *25*, 29, *41*, *42*, *71*, *75*
    2023, 12
Bayerische Staatsoper, 82n, 123n
Bechtolf, Erich, 136
Beijing, 46n
bel canto, 81, 115, 116, 119
    the term defined, 113–14
Bellini, Vincenzo, 115, 117
Bergen Festival, 105n
Bernac, Pierre, 107n
Boulez, Pierre, 105n
Braunschweig, 46n
Bravo-Casas, Germán, 13
Broadway, 106–7
Bromka, Elaine, 13
Budapest, 138
Buddhism, 37, 91–92, 98

cabaletta, 82–83
Callas, Maria, 114n
Canadian Opera Company, 104n
Carsen, Robert, 104, *108*
castrati, 117
Chéreau, Patrice, 105, *108*

Chicago
    Lyric Opera, 118n
Codex Manesse, *18*
conductors, 106
contracts, 101–2
Corelli, Franco, 113
Corfield, Tom, 13
Cornwall, 44
Covent Garden > Royal Opera House
Covid pandemic, 9, 47–48, 91, 137
Creutzinger, Matthias, 13

Davidsen, Lise, 13, 129–30
Denmark, 46n
Deutsche Oper, Berlin, 55n, 105n, 123n
Deutsche Oper am Rhein, Düsseldorf, 123n
directors
    and performers, 101–4, 107–8, 109
    their freedom to interpret, 107–8, 141
    the need for a 'solid concept', 108
    directors and conductors, 105, 109
Domingo, Plácido, 44n
Donizetti, Gaetano, 117, 123
Dortmund, 46n
Dresden, 35n, 123n
    SG as Tannhäuser there, *26*
    SG as Parsifal there, 91
    > *also* Semper Oper (Dresden)
Dudley Do-Right, 80
Dunbar, Ann, *75*
Düsseldorf, 123n

Eiche, Markus, 131–32
Eisenach, Thuringia, 19n
Elisabeth of Hungary, 19n
Epidaurus, 117

Fach and the *Fach* book, 90, 117, 123
Felsenstein, Walter, 55n, 64n
Finnish National Opera, Helsinki, 55n
Fiorito, John (SG's teacher), 89, 124
Florentine *Camerata*, 117
Foster, Catherine, 13, *41*, *133*, 133–34
Frankfurt am Main, 46n, 123n

fricative, 119
Friedrich, Götz, 54

Gateau Chocolat, Le, *29*
Gergiev, Valery, 106
glissando, 120
Globe Theatre, 117
Gluck, Christoph Willibald, 117
Glyndebourne Festival Opera, 44n
Gould, Stephen, *11, 22, 25, 85, 96, 127*
  personality, 7, 129, 135, 137
  how this book came to be written, 9
  illness and death, 12
  religious convictions, 12
  upbringing, 17
  approach to roles, 91
  vocal education, 107, 119, 124
  working method in rehearsal, 129
  on stage, 130
  open to new ideas, 130
  unfailing vocal technique, 131
  warm-up exercise, 131
  his last *Tristan*, 134
  professionalism, 136, 141
  guidelines for a singer, 138-39
Grundheber, Franz, 120, *121*
Gubanova, Ekaterina, 13, *30*, 135, *135*

Hairy Ape, The, 104n
Hamburg, 84, 118n
  State Opera, 55n
Handel, George Frideric, 115, 117
Haymarket, 117
Held, Alan, 82n
Heldentenor, 53, 55, 60, 82, 90, 117, 122, 123, 125
Henry the Fowler, 80
Herheim, Stefan, 105-6, *108*
Herlitzius, Evelyn, 46, *47*, *96*
Hermann, Hubertus, 13
Hilley, Clay, 12
Hole, James, 13
Holländer, Ioan, 136
Holstein, 123n
Hoskin, Niall, 13
Houtzeel, Stephanie, *75*

Jerusalem, Siegfried, 43n, 52-53
Jordan, Philippe, 90-91

Kampe, Anja, 82n
Kareol, 44
Kober, Axel, 129

Komische Oper, East Berlin, 55n, 64n
Konieczny, Tomasz, 136-37, *136*
Konwitschny, Franz, 43n,
Konwitschny, Peter, 43, 44, 82, 84
Kónya, Sándor, *122*, 123
Kratzer, Tobias, 21, 25, 29, 30, 107, *108*
kudzu, 83
Kupfer, Harry, 64, 129

Lancelot, 38, 69
Lang, Petra, 13, 46, *47*, 91, *138*, 138-39
La Scala, Milan, 123n
Latvian National Opera, Riga, 105n
Laudenbach, Manni, *29, 30*
Levine, James, 106
Linz, 28n, 105n
Liszt, Franz, 90n
Lloyd Webber, Andrew
  The Phantom of the Opera, 7, 103-4
Loki (Norse god), 52
London, 45, 123n
Ludwig IV, Margrave of Thuringia, 19n

Mahler, Gustav
  Eighth Symphony, 138
Malvolio (*Twelfth Night*), 54
Mama, La, 117
Mansouri, Lofti, 104n
Mehta, Zubin, 106
Meier, Waltraud, 43, 106
Melchior, Lauritz, 57n, 90, 118
Metropolitan Opera, New York, 52-53, 89n, 90, 113n, 118n, 123n
Midas, 52
Mielitz, Christine, 137
Millington, Barry, 13
minnesinger, 17, *18*
Moll, Kurt, 43, 106
Moriarty, John, 107
Mozart, 117, 123
  singing Mozart, 114
Munich, 10, 43, 82, 118n, 123n, 138
music as a form of communication, 47
musical theatre, 106-7

New England Conservatory, 107
New York, 89n
New York City Opera, 89n
Norwegian National Opera, 105n
Nuremberg, 43n

Olivero, Magda, 114
O'Neill, Eugene, 104

General Index

Ono, Kazushi, 82n
Opéra de la Bastille, 105n, 118n
Opéra de Paris, 27n, 123n
opera
  how it differs from spoken theatre, 102–3
  how it is more collaborative than symphonic music, 103
  orchestra, the singer's balance with, 81
Oslo, 105n
Osten, Vali von der, 118n

Padmore, Mark, 115
Pappano, Antonio, 44n
Paris, 138
Pauly, Simon, 13
Perryman, Roxanne, 13
Petri, Egon, 107n
Phillips, Julia, 13
plosive, 119
Popp, Lucia, 123n
portamento, 120
Prague, 35n

Quixote, Don, 69

Rattle, Simon, 91
Regietheater, 90n, 101
Richard Wagner Society of New York, 9
Robert Schumann Hochschule, Düsseldorf, 123n
Rocky and Bullwinkle Show, The, 80n
Rootering, Jan Hendrick, 118–19, *119*
Rossini, 114
Royal Opera House, Covent Garden, 55n, 61n, 123n
Rydl, Kurt, *97*

St Matthew Passion (Bach), 115
Saluzzo, 114n
salvation through the agency of a woman, 28–31, 80
Salzburg, 105n, 123n
Schager, Andreas, 12
Schenk, Otto, 52-53
Schnitzer, Petra-Maria, 123n
Schnorr von Carolsfeld, Ludwig, 35, *124*, 125
Schnorr von Carolsfeld, Malvine Garrigues, *124*
Schoenberg, 27, 90
Schopenhauer, 37, 91

The World as Will and Representation, 37n
Schröder, Simone, 75
Schröder-Devrient, Wilhelmine, 20
Scruton, Roger, 37
  Death-devoted Heart: Sex and the Sacred in Wagner's 'Tristan und Isolde', 37n
sea, 39
Sebastian (*Twelfth Night*), 54
Seiffert, Peter, *122*, 123
Semper Oper (Dresden), 26, 46n, 85, 96, 133, 138, 140
Shakespeare, 124
Shakespearian roles, 121
Shiva, 52
Siegel, Gerhard, 61
Sisyphus, 56
spinto, 123
squillo (or *squillando*), 116, 117–18, 122
Stein, Gertrude, 121
Stemme, Nina, 10, 44–46
Stockholm, 54n
Strauss, Richard, 46n, 115,
Stuttgart
  Staatsoper, 118n
Suzuki, Mr, 137
Sweden, 46n

Tebaldi, Renata, 114n
Theorin, Irène, 10, 46, *47*
Thielemann, Christian, 106
Thor (Norse god), 51
Tichatschek, Joseph, 20
Tischbein, Paul, *20*
Toccata Press, 13
Tokyo, 137, 138
  New National Theatre, 36
  Spring Festival, 137
Toronto, 104n
Tristram, 38
Twelfth Night, 54
twelve-note composition, 117

UK Wagner Society, 13
United States, 12, 107n

Vaughn, Tichina, *26*, 140
Veil of Maya, 44
Verdi, Giuseppe, 80, 123
  Il trovatore, 80n
verismo, 114, 123
Vienna, 10, 35
Vienna Court Opera, 35n

Vienna Staatsoper, 9, 123n, 136, 137, 138
Virgin Mary, 19, 21, 23
Virginia, 10
vocal technique, 113–25
    the need for a technique that is completely reliable, 113, 120, 124, 131
    coming through the orchestra, 115
    different types of tenor, 116
    vocalism changing with time, 117
    balance between the vocal column and consonants, 118, 119–20, 124–25
    stamina in Wagner, 118, 124
    portamento and *glissando*, 120
    aging, 121–23
    SG summarises his ideas on technique, 125
    SG's warm-up exercise, 131–32
Vogt, Klaus Florian, 12, 82n, *122*, 123
Völker, Franz, *122*n 123
Volle, Michael, 141

Wagley, Stephen, 13
Wagner, Katharina, 7, 13, 40, 46, 46n

Wagner News, 13
Wagner, Richard, 123
    as a revolutionary, 25
    the relationship between his life and his work, 98
    what he required of singers, 113–18, 124–25
    balance of words and music, 119–20
    auditioning and teaching singers, 124–25
Wagner, Wieland, 90
Wagner, Wolfgang, 90n
Weimar, 35n
Weitz, Ann, 13
Welser-Möst, Franz, 116–17, 136
Wesendonck, Mathilde, 37
Windgassen, Fritz, 118n
Windgassen, Wolfgang, 118, *119*, 123
'Workshop Bayreuth', 105

Zurich Opera House, 123n

Printed in the USA
CPSIA information can be obtained
at www.ICGtesting.com
JSHW011845020924
69160JS00003B/18